The Teacher's
ULTIMATE
STRESS MASTERY
Guide

I dedicate this book with deep love to my beloved father, Bill, who taught me how to use humor to buffer myself from the stressors of life; to my dear wife, Ronnie, whose patience, love, and kindness have enabled me to spend countless hours working on this book without feeling guilty; and to my wonderful children and granddaughter, Amie, Allison, Stacey, Lee, and Kenzi, who all graciously put up with my grumpiness and lack of attention as I focused so much of my time on meeting my deadlines!

The Teacher's ULTIMATE STRESS MASTERY Guide

77 Proven Prescriptions
to Build Your Resilience

JACK SINGER

A Joint Publication

CORWIN
A SAGE Company

ONTARIO
PRINCIPALS'
COUNCIL

For information:

Corwin
A SAGE Company
2455 Teller Road
Thousand Oaks, California 91320
(800) 233-9936
Fax: (800) 417-2466
www.corwinpress.com

SAGE Pvt. Ltd.
B 1/I 1 Mohan Cooperative
    Industrial Area
Mathura Road, New Delhi 110 044
India

SAGE Ltd.
1 Oliver's Yard
55 City Road
London EC1Y 1SP
United Kingdom

SAGE Asia-Pacific Pte. Ltd.
33 Pekin Street #02-01
Far East Square
Singapore 048763

Printed in the United States of America

Library of Congress Cataloging-in-Publication Data

Singer, Jack.
The teacher's ultimate stress mastery guide: 77 proven prescriptions to build your resilience/ Jack Singer.
      p. cm.
"A Joint Publication With the Ontario Principals' Council."
Includes bibliographical references and index.
ISBN 978-1-4129-7092-1 (cloth)
ISBN 978-1-4129-7093-8 (pbk.)
    1. Teachers—Job stress. 2. Stress management. I. Ontario Principals' Council. II. Title.

LB2840.2.S56 2010
371.1001'9—dc22   2009028985

This book is printed on acid-free paper.

09   10   11   12   13   10   9   8   7   6   5   4   3   2   1

Acquisitions Editor:	Arnis Burvikovs
Associate Editor:	Desirée A. Bartlett
Production Editor:	Veronica Stapleton
Copy Editor:	Codi Bowman
Typesetter:	C&M Digitals (P) Ltd.
Proofreader:	Dennis W. Webb
Indexer:	Sheila Bodell
Cover Designer:	Scott Van Atta

Contents

Preface

Knowledge without action is the greatest self-con of all.

—*Sharon Wegscheider Cruse, author*

You marvel at your teaching colleagues who seem to be calm and content, despite dealing with the exact same challenges and stressors that keep you tense and unhappy. You wonder how other teachers can bounce back after being berated by a belligerent parent or antagonized by an oppositional, defiant youngster in their class. You complain about the lack of administrative support in your school, yet some of your colleagues in the same school merrily charge on, without complaint. You worry about accountability demands, yet some of your colleagues seem unfazed by them.

Whether it's mastering new subject matter, addressing diverse student needs, teaching with the pressures of accountability, stretched budgets, implementing assessments, learning new technology, maintaining classroom order, managing time, or making sure that all students learn, the demands placed on teachers and administrators are increasing in number and intensity.

Compounding these demands, you are now required to wear the additional hats of a nurse, psychologist, social worker, and attorney. You are required to monitor medications, watch for diabetic and allergic reactions, manage confusing restraining orders on parents and step-parents, teach while students are texting one another, and deal with student behavioral challenges that their overwhelmed parents feel helpless to modify.

And then, when you can finally go home, besides grading papers, preparing for the next day, and taking care of your family's needs, you have to deal with the host of regional, national, world, economic, and weather crises that everyone else has to deal with. It's no wonder that teachers are at an extremely high risk for burnout and why low morale and job dissatisfaction are raging in our school systems.

Martin Haberman's (2004) review of the literature shows that stress levels among teachers and educational administrators have been rising dramatically over the years, and the average tenure for urban teachers is only 11 years. Furthermore, half of new teachers leave their jobs in five years or less (Corwin, 1973). Burnout has become a serious concern for teachers at all levels of tenure (Brock & Grady, 2000).

But not all teachers experience burnout and leave the profession. Are some people just better suited to deal with stress than others? Is there a stress-prone personality type that makes one more vulnerable to stressors? Can we learn how to increase the effectiveness of how we cope with the stressors that surround us? Can we actually learn skills that will buffer us against stressors and make us more resilient?

Obviously, the answers to these questions are critical when deciding whether you are going to complete a career in teaching or succumb to teacher burnout and leave the profession. How can you survive in this demanding and underappreciated field? This book will provide answers and show you how to develop resilience to the inevitable stressors that you will face during your teaching career.

Let's begin here with the story of Benita A., who was recognized in 2008 by *USA Today* as an All-USA teacher. Benita teaches high school juniors and seniors, with mixed ability students in each of her classes. There is not enough time in the day for Benita to accomplish everything she wants to. She works from 6:00 a.m. to 5:00 p.m. and then comes home to grade homework and several other activities. She says her greatest challenges are motivating her unmotivated students while trying to challenge highly motivated students, who are often stressed having to deal with their parents' expectations of all A's.

┌─ Good News! ─────────┐

This book is filled with practical, easy-to-learn tips (prescriptions) that teach you how to buffer yourself against stress and how to master the stressors that still manage to creep into your life. Success stories from teachers will also be provided so that you may consider adopting some of their secrets of success over the stressors involved in teaching.

Benita has found a marvelous way to work on both of these challenges simultaneously. Recognizing that her poorer performers suffer from lower self-esteem, expectations that they won't do well, and the it's-not-cool-to-make-A's syndrome, Benita does not separate her highly motivated, good students from her at-risk students.

Instead, Benita gets volunteers from her motivated group to work as student assistants, role models for the struggling students, helping them do their best. She finds that not only do the good students find this work rewarding, but also the other students realize that these "nerds" can be cool. An atmosphere of mutual respect develops.

Benita tells *all* of her students that they are capable of getting A's. Accordingly, she starts every student with an A+ at the beginning of the grading period. She let's them know that she will be there both before and after class for anyone in need of help and for informal study groups. She encourages a *team spirit* in her class. Additionally, Benita has instituted a unique, self-evaluation point system that each student completes at the end of each day with the following questions:

- Were you on time? (1 point)
- Did you bring your materials to class? (1 point)
- How well did you listen without interfering with others during the day? (2 points)
- Did you work until the bell or was your work finished early? (1 point)

Students see their point totals each day. Their grade slips only when they *lose* a point. So the students are accountable for their behavior and performance. Benita expects that *all* of her students are capable of performing well, thus instilling a *positive*, self-fulfilling prophecy in them. Amazingly, since she instituted this system, Benita has had *no disciplinary problems* in any of her classes. Furthermore, most of her students wind up with Bs or better! This brings to mind a quote from famous author John Stuart Mill:

> *A pupil from whom nothing is ever demanded which he cannot do never does all he can.*

Each chapter in this book will have a real-life example from a teacher, except Chapter 6, in which I will share information about myself and what I did to ward off the stressors of meeting the deadlines for finishing this book!

This book is intended to be a "rat-eared," self-help primer that you revisit often for precise prescriptions for not only mastering the stressors in your job and life, but also reminders of how you can be proactive and greatly reduce your vulnerability to those stressors. Ideally, you will learn how to *prevent* experiencing the symptoms of *distress* and burnout. In essence, you will develop a Teflon-like *resilience* to the stressors that will inevitably cross your path.

The behavioral prescriptions contained in this guide are all based on state-of-the-art research in the fields of *Cognitive Behavioral Therapy, Stress Mastery, Resilience Theory,* and the *New Positive Psychology for Authentic Happiness.*

In addition to the comments of nationally recognized teachers whom I have interviewed, much of my information is based on the many teacher clients I have treated over the past 33 years in my private and consulting practices. The goals here are to rivet your attention to the nuts and bolts of mastering stress and preventing burnout with easy-to-learn, proven strategies that *really work!*

Each chapter begins with a list of learning objectives and focuses on a real-life anecdote. You'll also find special features throughout the book, including "Good News" boxes, which direct you to practical actions you can take to lower your stress level, and "Stress Mastery Prescriptions," which are stress-management tools to help you take charge of your emotional well-being, in both the short and the long term. Finally, each chapter concludes with a specific action plan. Each action plan summarizes what you learned in the chapter and includes a checklist to help you integrate your new behavioral skills into your everyday repertoire. There are also several blank boxes available in each action plan so you can include additional behaviors and skills that you began as a result of reading that chapter. So keep this book close by and relax, knowing that there is an action plan available at the end of each chapter to keep you on target.

All of the Stress Mastery Prescriptions are listed together in Resource B for easy review, so you can pick and choose prescriptions as the need presents.

Although learning the exact sources of your stress and how to become more resilient to them is the basic purpose of this book, practicing your new skills is essential to success. With practice, you will succeed in developing new habits, which will help you insulate or *inoculate* yourself against the devastations of psychological burnout.

Have a highlighter and pen handy. Highlight and put asterisks next to the sections, descriptions, teacher stories, phrases, and action plans that affect your life and you will want to find again easily. Consider using a red pen to mark passages that give you hope, and write "Good News" in the margin.

Actually, there are many more than 77 proven behavioral prescriptions to help you succeed because many of them are multiple prescriptions and the text and many of the tables have additional prescriptions embedded in them. My goal is for this book to be a comfort to you, helping you to realize that there are behaviors that you can put into action immediately to overcome any issue or problem in your teaching career.

If you skip around, be sure to go back and read the sections you skipped because there are prescriptions scattered throughout each chapter, which you may want to put to use immediately. Choose new prescriptions to incorporate in your weekly routine and practice, practice, practice. Research shows that if you practice these skills consistently, you should see positive changes in about 21 days (Fishel, 2003).

Besides personal skills, the prescriptions also include suggestions to bring to your classroom and to share with your administrators. Because stress in the teaching profession is so pervasive, perhaps you can organize a teacher support group in your community so you can all share these ideas and learn what your colleagues have successfully done in their schools and lives to overcome their stress.

Although we are all victims of unfortunate, self-defeating, habitual patterns of setting ourselves up for distress and letting it get the best of us, we are certainly capable of breaking through the psychological shackles that have bound us since we were children to explore new ways of thinking and reacting that are positive and beneficial. For many of us, embracing change is risky, but those risks certainly have their rewards. You have many choices in life. Among them is choosing to change unfortunate beliefs, assumptions, and behaviors that have kept you trapped in a cocoon of unhappiness, stress, and despair. For many of you, choosing to make changes represents risk; however, most well-thought-out risks reap lifetime rewards. Robert Frost (1993) said it best:

> *Two roads diverged in a wood, and I—*
> *I took the one less traveled by,*
> *And that has made all the difference.*

From *The Road Not Taken and Other Poems,* by Robert Frost, p. 1, Dover Publications, Stanley Applebaum, Editor, 1993. Used with permission.

Enjoy this journey to health, success, and happiness. In many ways, your life depends on it.

Following the action plan, at the end of each chapter, there will be a references list.

REFERENCES

Brock, B. L., & Grady, M. L. (2000). *Rekindling the flame.* Thousand Oaks, CA: Corwin.

Corwin, R. G. (1973). *Organizational reform and organizational survival: The teacher corps as an instrument of educational change.* New York: Wiley.

Fishel, R. (2003). *Change almost anything in 21 days: Recharge your life with the power of over 500 affirmations.* Deerfield Beach, FL: Health Communications.

Frost, R. (1993). *The road not taken and other poems.* New York: Dover.

Haberman, M. (2004, January 9). *Teacher burnout in black and white.* Retrieved April 4, 2009, from http://www.altcert.org/Articles/PDF/Teacher%20Burnout%20in%20Black%20and%20White.pdf.

Acknowledgments

My hat goes off to all of the teachers with whom I consulted during my journey of joy while writing this book. My work with teachers for the past 33 years has filled me with admiration and inspiration. In particular, I acknowledge Benita A., Debbie L., Connie B., Mary C., Cheryl M., Ellie R., Debbie P., Brenda H., Rich M., Tommie M., and Mike L., the teachers who graciously gave of their time to share their secrets of success over stress.

I also want to acknowledge Arnis Burvikovs, senior editor at Corwin. Arnis provided the spark that encouraged me to write this book, and I will always be indebted to him for that. Finally, I am very grateful to Desirée Bartlett, associate editor at Corwin. Desirée continually had a patient and comforting ear when I called with technical questions, and she absolutely kept me from feeling overwhelmed.

Corwin gratefully acknowledges the contributions of the following individuals:

Diane Callahan, Science Teacher
Fairfield Middle School
Fairfield, OH

Toni Callahan, Retired Social Studies Teacher
Westmont Hilltop School District
Johnstown, PA

David Callaway, Eighth-Grade Language Arts Teacher
Rocky Heights Middle School
Highlands Ranch, CO

Emmalee Callaway, Second-Grade Discovery Teacher
Acres Green Elementary School
Parker, CO

About the Author

 **Dr. Jack Singer** is a professional psychologist who practices the specialties of clinical, sport, and organizational psychology. A proud member of the National Speakers Association, Dr. Jack is also a professional speaker and trainer, who has conducted training programs for educational associations, school systems, and Fortune 1000 companies from Miami to Malaysia. Jack has been awarded diplomate status from the American Academy of Behavioral Medicine and the Psychology Division of the National Institute of Sport Professionals, and he has taught in the psychology departments of seven universities, including an assistant professorship at the U.S. Air Force Academy.

The wide variety of his experience ranges from designing team-building re*treats* for school systems to training world-class athletes, and he even appeared on the "Here's Lucy" show with the queen of comedy herself. Jack understands the tremendous value of using humor as an antidote to stress and is renowned across the United States for his innovative work in bringing fun to the busy workplace.

A sought after media guest, Jack is called on frequently to comment on CNN, MSNBC, the Glenn Beck Show, Fox Sports, and ESPN, as well as talk radio shows throughout the United States and Canada. His articles appear in business, human resources, medical, and sports periodicals, and his consulting work has been featured in *USA Today*.

Jack has coauthored two previous books, his latest being *Dynamic Health*, and he also has produced several self-help programs, including hypnotic audios for raising self-esteem and another hypnotic series for athletes to maintain peak performance.

Jack has enjoyed wide acclaim for his powerful and funny keynote presentations, including "Powerful Prescriptions to Prevent Hardening of the Attitudes During Uncertain Times" and "How to Live Much Longer Than Your Kids Hoped You Would!" Regardless of the audience or presentation topic, Jack is committed to helping everyone he trains to add years to their lives while they add life to their years. For more information regarding Jack's in-service training and professional speaking services, visit his Web site at www.drjacksinger.com, contact him at 1–800–497–9880, or e-mail him at drjack@askdrjack.com

PART I

Understanding the Real Causes of Your Stress

1

How Stress Can Kick the Health Out of You

A critical shift in medicine has been the recognition that many of the damaging diseases of slow accumulation can be either caused or made far worse by stress.

—Robert Sapolsky (1998)

LEARNING OBJECTIVES

- I will be able to recognize the potential impact on my health from long-term stressors.
- I will understand the powerful mind and body connection.
- I will know how to calm myself quickly whenever I am feeling stressed.
- I will be able to cite the specific stressors at school and in my life that affect me on a regular basis.
- I will understand the concept of *eustress* and how some stress actually helps me to be successful in life.

Debbie L. embarked on her new teaching career, thrilled to be in a profession she always dreamed of. She was assigned to a junior high school in a rough area of town, where she was soon assaulted by a student, had a knife pulled on her, was followed home by a strange-acting man after attending a late faculty meeting, and even had a petition circulated against her by several of her teaching colleagues. Before long, Debbie's regular routine began with signing in at school, getting nauseous, and running to the bathroom. When she came home after teaching each evening, she had to have a couple of glasses of wine to calm down from the day. Did Debbie's stress end her teaching career? You'll see the rest of Debbie's story at the end of the chapter.

On June 6, 1983, "Stress!" was on the cover of *Time* magazine, and it was referred to as the "epidemic of the eighties" and the nation's primary health problem (American Institute of Stress [AIS], n.d.). Job stress was listed as, by far, the leading source of stress among Americans.

Let's move on to the end of 2007. On December 12, 2007, results from the American Psychological Association's (APA) annual survey of stress among the general public in the United States was released (APA, 2007). This "Stress in America" survey listed results from close to 2000 Americans, 18 and older, and the survey was conducted in both English and Spanish.

Most of those surveyed (79%) said that they could not avoid stress in their lives. A total of 77% of those surveyed experienced stress-related physical symptoms, including headaches, gastrointestinal (GI) problems, and unexplained fatigue. Nearly half of those surveyed (43%) blamed problems with their families or personal time on their stress levels (APA, 2007).

The survey was repeated in September 2008, with data gathered between June and August 2008 (APA, 2008). Nearly half (47%) of respondents reported increases in their stress levels since 2007. In the report, Dr. Katherine Nadal, APA's executive director for professional practice, said, "People's emotional and physical health is more vulnerable, given the high levels of stress in our country right now" (APA, 2008).

You can see from the prescriptions side of Table 1.1 that this book is filled with plenty of easy-to-learn remedies and buffers to help you ward off stressors and eradicate them once they are in place.

Notice that your stress-related symptoms are broken down into five categories: anxiety, depression, physical, behavior, and relationship symptoms. Most people have a combination of symptoms across all of these categories, and many studies show that folks with chronic anxiety or depressive symptoms, combined with hostility and cynicism, have double the risk of developing the diseases and symptoms listed under physical symptoms.

┌─ Good News! ─────────

Just because you are presently suffering from stress-related physical symptoms does not mean you are doomed to continue to suffer those symptoms. See Table 1.1 for a checklist of symptoms and the location in this book where you will find easy-to-learn prescriptions for eliminating those symptoms.

Table 1.1	Checklist of Potential Stress Symptoms and Self-Help Prescriptions That Really Work

Copy this table and check all of the symptoms that apply to you. Add any additional symptoms that you are experiencing. Note the chapters and resources where prescriptions to resolve those symptoms are discussed and visit Resource B to find additional prescriptions that also address these symptoms.

Anxiety Symptoms	Prescriptions
☐ Desperate ☐ Feeling as if you are losing control ☐ Frightened ☐ Irritable and frustrated ☐ Negative, self-defeating thinking ☐ Nervous, on edge, uptight ☐ Panicky ☐ Racing thoughts ☐ Sense of impending doom ☐ Worrying ☐ ☐ ☐	▢ *Recognize your Life Event Changes (see Chapter 2)* ▢ *Take charge of future life events (see Chapter 2)* ▢ *Relax your muscles (see Resource C)* ▢ *Recognize your distorted thoughts (see Chapter 3)* ▢ *Use the Thinking-Pattern Worksheet (TPW) (see Chapter 5)* ▢ *Realize that these symptoms are temporary, and they will lift once you take charge of your thinking and planning for the future (see Chapter 8)*
Depression Symptoms	*Prescriptions*
☐ Appetite changes ☐ Concentration difficulties ☐ Helplessness ☐ Hopelessness ☐ Indecisiveness ☐ Isolation and avoiding contacts ☐ Loss of confidence ☐ Loss of energy ☐ Loss of interests ☐ Loss of motivation ☐ Loss of sex drive ☐ Poor self-esteem	▢ *Recognize your distorted thoughts (see Chapter 3)* ▢ *Use the TPW (see Chapter 5)* ▢ *Use the Thought-Stopping Technique (see Chapter 5)* ▢ *Practice relaxation techniques (see Resource C)* ▢ *Be more assertive (see Chapter 4)* ▢ *Laugh each day (see Chapter 7)*

(Continued)

Table 1.1   (Continued)

Depression Symptoms	Prescriptions
☐ Sadness ☐ Sleeping changes ☐ Suicidal thoughts ☐ ☐ ☐	
Physical Symptoms	*Prescriptions*
☐ Agitation ☐ Chest and/or muscle tightness ☐ Diarrhea or constipation ☐ Feeling dizzy or lightheaded ☐ Feeling tired and weak ☐ Headaches, migraine and tension ☐ Muscle tightness, pain, and spasms ☐ Racing heart ☐ Restlessness or jumpiness **Reduced disease immunity may lead to or inflame a host of diseases, including** ☐ Asthma ☐ Back and neck pain ☐ Cancer ☐ Cardiovascular disorders, including high blood pressure and chest pain ☐ Dermatological disorders ☐ Diabetes ☐ Gastrointestinal disorders	*Practice relaxation techniques (see Resource C)* *Practice assertiveness skills (see Chapter 4)* *Practice stress hardiness (see Chapter 6)*

Physical Symptoms	Prescriptions
❏ Headaches ❏ ❏ ❏	
Behavior Symptoms	*Prescriptions*
❏ Anger and hostility ❏ Harmful habits (overeating, use of substances, smoking, gambling, overspending) ❏ Impatience ❏ Impulsivity ❏ Irritability ❏ Rapid speech ❏ Resentment ❏ Procrastination ❏ Withdrawal ❏ ❏ ❏	❏ *Practice relaxation techniques (see Resource C)* ❏ *Practice assertiveness skills (see Chapter 4)* ❏ *Practice stress hardiness skills (see Chapter 6)*
Relationship Symptoms	*Prescriptions*
❏ Intimacy issues ❏ Lack of assertiveness ❏ Not listening to partner's needs ❏ Short fuse with partner or friends ❏ Parenting disagreements ❏ Poor communications ❏ Power struggles ❏ ❏ ❏	❏ *Practice active-listening skills (see Chapter 4)* ❏ *Practice assertiveness skills (see Chapter 4)*

Take care of your emotional health by taking care of your physical health. Consider visiting a licensed naturopathic physician to learn about foods and natural supplements that have been proven to reduce and prevent stress. The following are examples of healthy habits that have been shown to directly impact moods and stress levels: keep your blood sugar low with frequent, smaller meals that include protein; eat light at night; get ample sleep; avoid alcohol, caffeine, and tobacco; load up on antioxidant-rich foods, and keep your weight in the normal range for your age and height.

There are also potential emotional warning signs of stress-related burnout that are specific for teachers, including the following:

- Difficulty sleeping well on Sunday evenings,
- Feeling like not going to work and calling in sick,
- Having difficulty concentrating on tasks,
- Feeling overwhelmed by the workload and/or having a sense of inadequacy to handle the tasks assigned,
- Withdrawing from colleagues or engaging in conflict-filled relationships with coworkers, and
- Having a general feeling of irritation regarding school.

TALES OF A SABER-TOOTHED TIGER

A large body of evidence suggests that stress-related disease emerges, predominantly, out of the fact that we so often activate a physiological system that has evolved for responding to acute physical emergencies, but we turn it on for months on end, worrying about mortgages, relationships and promotions.

—Robert Sapolsky (1998)

Hans Seyle (1976), a Canadian physician and researcher, known as the "Father of Stress," defined stress as "the nonspecific response of the body to any demand" (p. 1). So stress is the feeling we get in response to any *stressor* (Seyle, 1976), whether it takes place at school or at home. Stressors throw your body out of balance, for example, an injury, illness, or pain. The stress response is part of your body's automatic attempt to restore balance, referred to as *homeostasis*. But it is critical to understand that for humans stressors also include beliefs, fears, worries, anticipation of something bad happening, and anything in our thinking that provokes the stress response. As you will learn throughout this book, these stressors are strictly under our control, and we can eliminate them once we understand them.

Of course, our bodies have been hot-wired genetically to deal with stressors involved in physical danger as a matter of survival. Visualize a caveman (or woman) coming out of the cave one morning, stretching, and contemplating the day's tasks. As our friend looks around, he spots a hungry saber-toothed tiger 20 yards away. This recognition of a serious danger throws the brain into emergency mode through the *sympathetic nervous system* (SNS), genetically programmed to prepare him for the fight, flight, or freeze response to this stressor. The SNS is so named because it provides a *sympathy* link between our perceptions and thoughts and the feelings in our internal organs.

Once he sees the tiger and thinks about the danger, the caveman's SNS automatically turns on several systems in his body, which begin the process of adapting to and dealing with this potentially life-threatening stressor. The resultant stress response includes the following actions:

- *Blood* that would be completing the digestive process moves away from the GI system to the external muscles. During this emergency stress response, there is no time for the slow process of digestion; plus, this would require energy that would serve better in the muscles for reacting in the fight, flight, or freeze response to the stressor.
- *Perspiration* increases to cool the body, which helps it burn more energy for fight, flight, or freeze responses.
- *Muscles*, particularly in the arms, legs, back, and neck, tighten to be ready to act quickly.
- *Glucose* pours into the bloodstream to provide instant energy for the fight, flight, or freeze reaction to this stressor. But how does the caveman's body deliver the glucose to the critical muscles as quickly as possible?
- His *heart rate, blood pressure,* and *respiratory rate* all increase to transport nutrients and oxygen at greater rates to his brain to make decisions and to his muscles to prepare for action.
- *Adrenalin* from the adrenal glands pours into the bloodstream to keep him alert.
- *Cortisol*, known as the stress hormone, is released to increase energy and strengthen the body's defenses.
- *Blood clotting* chemicals spring to action in the bloodstream to prevent excess bleeding in case there is an injury that takes place during the fight, flight, or freeze response.
- The *immune system* is inhibited. This is fine for the short term, when you don't need your immune system to be making antibodies to protect you from viruses and diseases that may threaten your health or life months down the road. However, this is a critical reaction because the long-term inhibition of the immune system from continual exposure to stressors (and continually switching on the SNS) suppresses the immune function and strips the body of its natural protection from diseases.

You can appreciate the remarkable adaptation of the human body through evolution to deal with obvious life-threatening and dangerous emergencies, but because these emergencies were infrequent when man first existed, the system was designed to switch on *infrequently*. Grazing animals, for example, have to switch on this nervous system periodically when they are threatened by predators, but the encounter is usually relatively short-lived, and the animal then relaxes and goes about its business of grazing.

For humans, the SNS also responds to situations and events that we interpret and *think* about—typically not emergencies or threats. Unfortunately, our brain does not recognize the difference between a real threat and one that we anticipate by vividly imagining something awful or sad happening to us in the future.

For example, if I ask you to use all of your senses to visualize yourself biting into a juicy lemon right now, you will begin to salivate automatically and your glands secrete a base solution into your mouth (saliva) to counteract the acid from the lemon. So the brain takes its directions from your thoughts and images, even though what you are visualizing and thinking about is not actually occurring.

Think about what may be a typical day for you: You had a rough day at school, with several of your students displaying disruptive behavior as the rest of the class laughed in amusement. You got word from your non-supportive principal that because of budget cuts, your teaching assistant's position will be eliminated by the end of the week, and by the way, a disgruntled parent insisted on a conference with you after school today. You said to yourself,

> *I'm having enough trouble trying to explain their homework assignment without these disruptions. They'll never understand how to do their homework if I don't get this done before the bell rings. Once my assistant leaves, my workload will be unmanageable. I am in no mood to deal with this parent after school today. My principal never supports me. This isn't fair. I don't know what to do.*

Each of these anxiety-producing thoughts, beliefs, and predictions represents a *psychological* stressor that has evolved relatively recently in our evolutionary development. Importantly, each is a potential upset to our internal system, switching on the SNS the same way that a real emergency does.

THE INCREDIBLE MIND-BODY CONNECTION

> *The evidence is growing stronger that states of mind can affect physical health.*

> —Goleman and Gurin (1993)

As I mentioned, our brains do not differentiate real dangers from those we craft in our minds when we worry about actual or anticipated disturbing events in our lives. Each physiological response to life-threatening stressors serves a critical, life-preserving purpose, as noted in the nine examples earlier; but because our bodies were designed only to activate this SNS infrequently and when our lives are *actually* in danger, the daily switching on that so many of us experience because of our worrying puts tremendous strain on the system. The result is the potential for physiological damage. Therefore, as scientists Robert Sapolsky (1998) and Hans Seyle (1976) describe, each adaptive response has a debilitating consequence for the human body when it is triggered frequently by worries and concerns:

- *Blood* continually leaving the GI tract to flow into the muscles of the legs and arms preparing for the fight, flight, or freeze reaction can lead to vomiting, energy loss, and chronic *digestive problems*, including gastritis and irritable bowel syndrome.
- People who are constantly under stress frequently have embarrassing *perspiration issues*, including dampness when shaking hands.
- *Muscles* continually tightening up can lead to muscle spasms, tension, and *pain*, particularly in the neck and back. In addition, chronic muscle tension contributes to migraine and tension headaches, jaw clenching, and fatigue.
- *Glucose* spilling into the bloodstream often contributes to *diabetes* and other endocrine disorders.
- If your *blood pressure* rises to 180/130 when you're facing someone who is threatening your life, your body is reacting appropriately, but if your pressure is 180/130 several mornings a week as you get ready to go to school, you are at great risk for chronic cardiovascular problems and *hypertension* (high blood pressure), causing potential consequences such as circulation problems or heart and kidney damage. Chronic hypertension also causes feelings of *nervousness and pressure.*
- The chronic worrier or anxious person triggers the brain to spill *adrenalin* continuously into the bloodstream. Because a function of adrenalin is to keep you alert, a side effect of having too much adrenalin residing in your bloodstream is *insomnia*. This is why so many highly stressed people have sleeping difficulties.
- Although cortisol is necessary to prepare the muscles for vigorous reactions in the face of danger, the continual release of cortisol into the bloodstream blocks the removal of certain acids and breaks down lean tissue to convert to sugar for energy in the survival scenario. This causes *ulcerations* in the lining of the stomach, which is why so many people diagnosed with ulcers are people suffering from chronic stress. Long-term, chronic release of stress hormones like cortisol damages the body in many ways and leads to many diseases.
- Frequent *blood clotting* puts a person at a great risk for *stroke or heart attack.*
- *Suppressing your immune functioning* because of the constant switching on of the SNS can lead to disastrous consequences in terms of fighting infections and protecting you from *immune system disorders,*

including allergies, arthritis, AIDS, lupus, some cancers, the common cold, and the flu.

We can literally look at any major system in the body and find evidence of symptoms being caused in whole or in part by too much activation of the stress-response system, rather than by the invasion of disease-causing bacteria or cancers. As Sapolsky (1998) explains it, "If you repeatedly turn on the stress response, or if you cannot appropriately turn off the stress response at the end of a stressful event, the stress response can eventually become nearly as damaging as some stressors themselves" (p. 16).

As you would expect, much research has linked stress with many chronic diseases and with the many of the leading causes of death, including heart disease, cancer, stroke, lung diseases, and of course, suicide (Sapolsky, 1998).

Stress also impacts cholesterol levels, platelet activation (causing heart attacks), and often shortens life span. Mental stressors, such as loneliness, depression, and isolation, are also associated with serious illnesses and shortened life span. Sleep disorders negatively impact the immune system and life span, and because stress is one of the main causes of the inability to fall and stay asleep, you can see the tremendous impact of stress on our overall health and longevity!

Physiological Symptoms Associated With Stresses Inherent in Teaching

In their book, *Stress in Teachers*, Dunham and Varma (1998) cite many studies showing a clear relationship between the stressors inherent in teaching and physiological symptoms. The prevalence of stress-related symptoms for teachers is (in descending order):

- physical exhaustion/fatigue,
- skeleto-muscular tension/pains,
- heart symptoms and high blood pressure,
- headaches,
- digestive disorders,
- respiratory difficulties,
- sleep disturbances, and
- voice loss.

It is important to understand that the stressors we face are not actually provoked by the events that take place in our lives daily but *how we interpret* and think about those events—what we say to ourselves about those events. We can set off our emergency response by *simply thinking about* these events or anticipating potential problems befalling us in the future. Consider your stress when your administrator tells you that you'll be taking a test next month to determine whether you will be retained in the school. Will you be worried about that test, even thought it is weeks away? Simply *anticipating* a problem can trigger the SNS to switch on.

A variety of sources, including the AIS (n.d.), estimate that 75% to 90% of the patients who arrive at the family practice or internist's office are suffering from stress-related physical symptoms.

This is no surprise. Just look at common phrases in our everyday language: *I am worried sick. My job is a pain in the neck. Sometimes I can't stomach some of my students.*

Perhaps you are aware that every drug company uses placebos (fake pills) in their research on real drugs. The companies need to prove that their drug has major effects beyond those produced in the minds of the patients who believe they are being given a drug to treat their symptoms. Hundreds of studies have determined that the optimistic, positive attitudes that patients have when their doctor prescribes something that "should really help you" (even though it was a benign sugar pill), lead to symptom reduction (Sapolsky, 1998; Seligman, 1998). Examples of conditions treated effectively with placebos are allergies, depression, migraine headaches, and alcohol dependence.

Besides the diseases and disorders listed previously that are caused or made worse by the impact of chronic stress, people often get themselves into more trouble when they try to cope with their stress: Alcoholism, substance abuse, and chronic smoking are common coping methods people use to modify their stress. Psychotropic medications, such as antidepressants and tranquilizers, are being prescribed in record numbers. You have much more control over your physical health than you realize. Research shows that more than half of the people hospitalized in the United States could have prevented their symptoms by changing their lifestyles (Charlesworth & Nathan, 1984).

Phew! Let's all take a deep breath here . . . literally—*Take a nice deep breath here*—That alone will begin to calm you. Yes, I know . . . the statistics you just reviewed are frightening, but whatever your stress level, you are *not* hopelessly destined to get sick or die from the stressors in your life. Although exposure to chronic or repeated stressors can *potentially* make you ill or increase your *risk* of getting a disease, such exposure *does not* automatically lead to illness. Many teachers under the same stress as you do not

---

Good News!

Because we know from the placebo effect that your mind can visualize both positive and negative images and respond accordingly, you can learn to consistently visualize *positive, healthy images,* and as a result, you can avoid many of the physical and emotional consequences of the potential stressors in your life.

---

get sick. How can that be? Can we learn how to increase the effectiveness of how we cope with the stressors that surround us? We will examine these questions as we go along.

What we do know is that suffering from stress does increase your *risk* of getting physically sick, and if you already have a disease, stress increases the probability of your defenses collapsing, thus setting off more symptoms. But *you* ultimately have control over how you will internalize your thoughts and beliefs about these stressors, and those thoughts and beliefs are the keys to mastering stress.

Practice breathing through your diaphragm. Put your hands on your stomach and breathe deeply so that your hands move out when you inhale and move back in when you exhale. If your hands are not moving and only your shoulders and chest move when you breathe deeply, you are engaging in shallow, less relaxing breathing. You can easily teach yourself to breathe through your diaphragm with practice.

SOME STRESS IS ACTUALLY *GOOD* FOR YOU

People are not disturbed by things, but by their perception of things.

—Epictetus, Greek philosopher

We know that too much chronic stress can actually kill you, but did you know that too *little* stress is also bad for you? Hans Seyle (1976) differentiated two kinds of stress: *distress* and *eustress*. Distress is obviously the harmful, unpleasant stress, and eustress is good stress, from exciting events, job promotions, a new class to teach that you were bidding for, and so on.

Although the body reacts to eustress in exactly the same way as it does to distress, eustress causes much less damage. Why is that? *It's because it's never the stressor that's the problem;* rather, it's how you interpret it and what you say to yourself about that stressor that determines whether the resultant stress experience is good or bad.

Even if you have many eustress experiences in your life, such as purchasing a new home, getting married, the birth of a baby, and taking a vacation, if you worry that these events will change your life in a negative way, the resultant stress will be felt as distress. For example, you are excited about the upcoming birth of a child but incessantly worry about how you will balance taking care of a newborn in your already hectic life.

Too little stress leaves most people bored and tired. It takes a certain amount of stress to keep alert, stay motivated, think creatively, solve problems, and keep your self-confidence high. In addition, gross motor skills and reaction time work best with a manageable level of stress. Think about the times you were so relaxed that you just couldn't muster the energy to go to the gym or even do a crossword puzzle. *Too little stress* cuts into your motivation and productivity; but *too much stress* cuts into your motivation, productivity, *and* your health!

Recognize that you can live with a certain amount of stress in your life and that it may even be beneficial to you.

The best balance is achieved by managing the way you deal with each stressor that comes along, rather than trying to eliminate each from your life altogether—a feat you most likely cannot accomplish anyway. As an example, embracing the change that comes with a new curriculum is a good thing, rather than finding reasons to debate the new curriculum because you fear change and are imagining how much more work is involved for you to adapt the curriculum changes.

Ask yourself what calm people do to maintain their stress levels. Examples of answers to that question are jogging or walking each morning before work, making time for lunch each day with a calm friend or colleague, and reading articles or the rest of this book on how to master the stresses in life.

Using Table 1.2, you can check off specific coping skills that you would like to learn using this book. Each of these skills is also directed at helping you to ward off stress and eradicate the stress you currently find yourself under. Make a copy of this table and check off the skills you learn as you go along.

Table 1.2 Checklist of Teacher Coping and Buffer Skills
Copy this and check off each skill as you accomplish it. These are discussed in detail throughout the book.
Coping and Buffer Skills I Need to Work On
❐ Develop a strong sense of self-esteem and feel good about myself in general
❐ Be able to quickly determine when I am under stress (e.g., the symptoms may be hidden in frequent illnesses, vague pains, increased intake of alcohol or cigarettes, unusual weight gain or loss, or impulsive behaviors)
❐ Understand when I need to delay making changes in my life
❐ Recognize when my thinking is negative and/or distorted
❐ Have a series of relaxation exercises built into my week
❐ Take relaxing time for myself each week
❐ Understand if I have personality traits that make me vulnerable to stress and practice modifying those traits
❐ Remain optimistic regardless of circumstances
❐ Develop psychological hardiness skills to ward off stress
❐ Make sure I find funny things to laugh at each week
❐ Assert myself and use good listening and communication skills
❐ Set realistic goals for myself
❐ Practice acts of forgiveness, volunteerism, and help a stranger in line or in traffic
❐ Have exercise and healthy diet habits
❐ Have a gratifying visit with someone who is special in my life

Remember Debbie, our junior high school teacher? She embarked on her career by being nauseated shortly after arriving at school and running to the bathroom. She had plenty of physical and emotional reasons to quit teaching, didn't she? But Debbie viewed this awful start to her teaching career as a challenge. She thought long and hard about how she could get both her students and her faculty colleagues to embrace her. In her own words,

> *I jumped in headfirst and took on all kinds of extra duties for the kids. I did the yearbook, took the kids on amazing field trips, entered them into all kinds of fun contests, which they won, and pretty much did everything I could for the students.*

Debbie's students and colleagues began to give her positive feedback. Debbie began to enjoy coming to school each day. In fact, she was so successful that she won the Teacher-of-the-Year award for her school.

You see, Debbie decided to manage the way she interpreted and dealt with situations she could not change and focus on where she could have an impact. She couldn't please every student, and she couldn't put the school in a better neighborhood. But she could focus on helping her students have a much better school experience than they were having prior to her arrival.

In subsequent chapters, you will learn how to manage, interpret, and talk to yourself about the stressors in your life so that you can truly control your stress level.

Stay fit. Run, bike, swim, walk, or hike each week. Aerobic (heart rate increasing) exercise releases endorphins. Other ways to benefit from exercise are dancing, gardening, or raking leaves. You don't have to engage in vigorous activity to benefit.

As was noted in the Preface, each chapter in this book will conclude with an action plan, which will tie back to the learning objectives for stress mastery for that chapter. Having a checklist action plan will help you to keep you on track for practicing your new stress mastery skills.

ACTION PLAN FOR STRESS MASTERY

Table 1.3	My Action Plan for Stress Mastery

Check each one when you've accomplished it.	
New Behavior	*What I Did and the Date Accomplished*
☐ Whenever I am feeling stressed or overwhelmed, I will calm myself by taking a series of slow, deep breaths in through my nostrils and out through my mouth. ☐ ☐ ☐	What I did: Date accomplished:
☐ I will not get overwhelmed by worrying about stress. I will tell myself that I can live with some stress and actually use it to my benefit. ☐ ☐ ☐	What I did: Date accomplished:
☐ I will embrace change, rather than resist it, and look for ways that change will lead to positive outcomes. ☐ ☐ ☐	What I did: Date accomplished:
☐ I will list all of the stressors that are currently affecting me related to my job, and then I will find something positive to say about as many of these stressors as possible. ☐ ☐ ☐	What I did: Date accomplished:
☐ I will list positive stressors in my life that actually help me (eustress). ☐ ☐ ☐	What I did: Date accomplished:

REFERENCES

American Institute of Stress. (n.d.). *America's number one health problem.* Retrieved April 10, 2009, from http://www.stress.org/Americas.htm.

American Psychological Association. (2007, October 24). *Stress is a major health problem in the U.S., warns APA.* Retrieved April 10, 2009, from http://www.apa.org/releases/stressproblem.html.

American Psychological Association. (2008, October 7). *APA poll finds women bear brunt of nation's stress, financial downturn.* Retrieved April 10, 2009, from http://www.apa.org/releases/women-stress1008.html.

Charlesworth, E. A., & Nathan, R. A. (1984). *Stress management: A comprehensive guide to wellness.* New York: Ballantine Books.

Dunham, J., & Varma, V. (Eds.). (1998). *Stress in teachers: Past, present, and future.* London: Whurr.

Goleman, D., & Gurin, J. (Eds.). (1993). *Mind body medicine.* Yonkers, NY: Consumer Report Books.

Helpguide.org. (n.d.). *Understanding stress.* Retrieved June 4, 2009, from http://www.helpguide.org/mental/stress_signs.htm.

Sapolsky, R. (1998). *Why zebras don't get ulcers.* New York: Freeman.

Seligman, M. E. (1998). *Learned optimism.* New York: Pocket Books.

Seyle, H. (1976). *The stress of life.* New York: Ballantine Books.

2

How Life Events and Changes Can Impact Stress and Illness

As individuals, we have different needs and differing abilities to adjust to life. However, if we want a greater share of happiness from life, we would do well to honestly examine our life patterns and to adjust them accordingly to allow ourselves more room to relax, reflect, and become more responsible for all our activities.

—Matthew Culligan (quoted in Culligan & Sedlacek, 1976)

LEARNING OBJECTIVES

- I will understand how engaging in multiple life changes during a 12-month time span may impact my stress level.
- I will use the Recent Life Changes Questionnaire (RLCQ) every 6 months to determine how many points I have accumulated.
- I will recognize when my total RLCQ points are reaching a critical range and will then delay making further changes for at least six months.

(Continued)

(Continued)

- I will categorize the stressors I am encountering in my teaching job according to whether they are important, unimportant, changeable, or unchangeable and use coping prescriptions relevant for each category.
- I will check off the coping prescriptions for each of my stressors and practice those prescriptions daily.

Connie B. taught in a middle school, and this had been a particularly difficult year for her. Following a long illness, her mother died, and six months later, her husband said he was divorcing her. Both of these events happened to her soon after she began taking classes in the evenings, working toward a master's degree.

Soon, she was suffering from depression, anxiety, and fear related to losing her two most important support systems in six months. This depression manifested itself in sleeping difficulties and exhaustion, making getting to school on time and teaching a grueling task for her. Connie was feeling overwhelmed and helpless. She contemplated quitting. Although she didn't know how she would earn a living, she thought that getting away from the job would relieve most of her stress. What happened to Connie? Read on to find out.

In their now famous and widely published studies, Dr. Thomas Holmes and his colleague, Dr. Richard Rahe (1967a, 1967b), determined that specific events in people's lives tended to cause predictable levels of stress, and these events all had a common thread—the necessity to change their lives in some way (Holmes & Rahe, 1967a, 1967b). For example, changing jobs demands making changes in one's life and, therefore, is stress provoking. In Connie's situation, losing a parent and getting divorced forced her to make major adjustments in her life. Even embarking on a much-anticipated evening educational program required adjustments, thus adding to her stress.

Dr. Mark Miller and Dr. Richard Rahe (1997) revised the social readjustment rating scale in 1997 and retitled it as the Recent Life Changes Questionnaire (RLCQ), which is found in Table 2.1.

As you can see, the RLCQ assigns a number of points to various events in a person's life according to the amount of change and adjustment that event demands. These are called life change units (LCUs). The higher the LCU score (i.e., the more changes that are occurring in people's lives), the greater the risk of developing *distress* (strain) and, therefore, stress-related illnesses or emotional problems. Interestingly, many of the items on the questionnaire seem like they would lead to *eustress* (Seyle, 1976), such as getting married, taking a vacation, or a job promotion. But, as you can imagine, each of these life events also requires a lot of adjusting and, therefore, can

Table 2.1   The Recent Life Changes Questionnaire (RLCQ)

Health	
❏ An injury or illness that	
☐ Kept you in bed a week or more or sent you to the hospital	74
☐ Was less serious than above	44
❏ Major dental work	26
❏ Major change in eating habits	27
❏ Major change in sleeping habits	26
❏ Major change in your usual type and/or amount of recreation	28
Work	
❏ Change to a new type of work	51
❏ Change in your work hours or conditions	35
❏ Change in your responsibilities at work	
☐ More responsibilities	29
☐ Fewer responsibilities	21
☐ Promotion	31
☐ Demotion	42
☐ Transfer	32
❏ Trouble at work	
☐ With your boss	29
☐ With coworkers	35
☐ With persons under your supervision	35
☐ Other work troubles	28
❏ Major business adjustment	60
❏ Retirement	52
❏ Loss of job	
☐ Laid off from work	68
☐ Fired from work	79
❏ Correspondence course to help you in your work	18
Home and Family	
❏ Major change in living conditions	42
❏ Change in residence	
☐ Move in the same town or city	25
☐ Move to a different town, city, or state	47

(Continued)

Table 2.1	(Continued)	
❏ Change in family get-togethers		25
❏ Major change in health or behavior of a family member		55
❏ Marriage		50
❏ Pregnancy		67
❏ Miscarriage or abortion		65
❏ Gain of a new family member		
☐ Birth of a child		66
☐ Adoption of a child		65
☐ A relative moving in with you		59
❏ Spouse beginning or ending work		46
❏ Child leaving home		
☐ To attend college		41
☐ Because of marriage		41
☐ Because of other reasons		45
❏ Change in arguments with spouse		50
❏ In-law problems		38
❏ Change in the marital status of your parents		
☐ Because of divorce		59
☐ Because of remarriage		50
❏ Separation from spouse		
☐ Because of work		53
☐ Because of marital problems		76
☐ Because of divorce		96
❏ Birth of a grandchild		43
❏ Death of spouse		119
❏ Death of other family member		
☐ Child		123
☐ Sibling		102
☐ Parent		100
Personal and Social		
❏ Change in personal habits		26
❏ Beginning or ending school or college		38

Personal and Social	
❐ Change of school or college	35
❐ Change in political beliefs	24
❐ Change in religious beliefs	29
❐ Change in social activities	27
❐ Vacation	24
❐ New, close, personal relationship	37
❐ Engagement to marry	45
❐ Girlfriend or boyfriend problems	39
❐ Sexual difficulties	44
❐ Falling out of a close personal relationship	47
❐ An accident	48
❐ Minor violation of the law	20
❐ Being held in jail	75
❐ Death of a close friend	70
❐ Major decision regarding your immediate future	51
❐ Major personal achievement	36
Financial	
❐ Major change in finances	
☐ Because of increased income	38
☐ Because of decreased income	60
☐ Because of investment and/or credit difficulties	56
❐ Loss or damage of personal property	43
❐ Moderate purchase	20
❐ Major purchase	37
❐ Foreclosure on a mortgage or loan	58
My Total Points for Events Taking Place in My Life in the Last 12 Months	

Reprinted from *The Journal of Psychosomatic Research, Vol. 43,* Mark Miller and Richard Rahe, "Life changing scaling for the 1990s," pp. 279–292, 1997, with permission from Elsevier Publishing.

ultimately cause strain. You can score up to 199 points and still be relatively insulated from stress consequences.

So take an objective look at Table 2.1, and consider your life over the *past 12 months*. Put a check mark in the box next to any of the events that have occurred in your life and then total your LCU points, recording your score at the bottom.

In multiple studies (Hawkins, Davies, & Holmes, 1957; Holmes & Masuda, 1970; Holmes & Rahe, 1967b; Miller & Rahe, 1997), a clear relationship was established between the number of LCUs from events occurring over the previous 12 months and the onset of a disease, illness, or even being involved in an accident in the subsequent 12 months. So scores from the past 12 months predict stress-related outcomes in the next 12 months.

YOUR RECENT LIFE CHANGES SCORE AND ITS INTERPRETATIONS

Life events on the Holmes and Rahe scale are not necessarily good or bad. They are simply times of extra strain.

—Keith Sedlacek (quoted in Culligan & Sedlacek, 1976)

Low LCU Score (0 to 199)

If your score falls in this range, your life changes in the past 12 months are relatively few in number and, therefore, relatively low in requirements for adjusting to change. Because of this low level of recent life changes, your risk for illness or an accident over the next year is also low. Only 10% of individuals in this range of life change stress become ill in the subsequent 12 months.

In fact, if you score in this range, you might find yourself bored, irritable, and easily distracted. Therefore, consider adding some new challenges to your life. For example, take up a new hobby or learn something new.

Moderate LCU Score (200 to 299)

Most Americans report a moderate level of recent life changes, and these changes are indicative of a moderate level of strain. Each year, most Americans tend to experience some changes involving their work, living conditions, family and personal lives, and in their financial circumstances. Approximately 30% of those who experience a moderate LCU score will go on to develop a stress-related illness (physical or emotional) or accident in the next 12 months. Furthermore, the research suggests that this illness or accident will likely be one of moderate severity. If you score in this range, you probably find life interesting, challenging, and active most of the time. You may feel bored at times and stressed at other times.

Elevated LCU Score (300 to 449)

A yearly LCU score in this range is considered elevated and is associated with an elevated risk for an upcoming illness or accident. For persons in this range, approximately 50% will likely experience an illness or accident over the following year. More than one illness may also occur, and some of these illnesses may be severe. The strain on the body from elevated life changes can impair, among other things, normal immune function. For example, if you fall in this range, you may first develop allergies, then a cold, and this could progress into pneumonia.

High LCU Score (450 and higher)

A high LCU score means not only that many life changes have taken place in the past 12 months, but also that some of these changes had very high stress point values. Dr. Miller and Dr. Rahe (1997) refer to such high scores as a high-stress load, and they call it a "life crisis." Persons experiencing a life crisis have a 65% chance of developing one or more illnesses and/or accidents in the next 12 months. If your score falls in this category, put off any new changes you are contemplating to give your body and mind time to recoup. Let's say you have many LCU points and you are thinking about changing jobs, moving out of state, or even getting married. It may be best to delay those major changes until you have calmed down from the effects of the recent changes in your life.

You should also make sure that you engage in exercise, proper nutrition, relaxation exercises, and many of the other prescriptions you'll find in this book to help you to manage your stress level, regardless of how high it is at that time in your life.

As you can imagine, this questionnaire is actually an *underestimate* of your stress because there are other events *not* listed on the RLCQ, which may have impacted your life and caused major changes for you over the past 12 months. For example, as I am writing this book, there is a new wave of stress-provoking events taking a toll on Americans: an economic recession, the bottom falling out of the housing and stock markets, record bank repossessions, the threat of global terrorism, the wars in Iraq and Afghanistan, and more and more natural disasters being attributed to the effects of global warming. None of these life-adjusting changes is represented in the RLCQ, so please understand that whenever you fill out the questionnaire, your score is most likely an *underestimate* of your actual stress level.

Many life-changing events happen to us without warning and are not included on the questionnaire. For example, as I was working on this chapter, my son walked in the door and announced that he was in an accident with our new car! Here is an example of a life change thrust on me without warning and not part of the RLCQ. I have to get estimates, rent a replacement car to use while mine is being repaired, worry about my insurance rates, plus make sure that my son isn't traumatized by the whole affair!

The 2008 American Psychological Association's (APA) annual "Stress in America" survey, released in October 2008, found that 80% of Americans cited money and the economy as the top stressors they faced. Family health problems and job security fell closely behind and were in many ways related to the money and economy stressors. These life changes are not directly taken into account on the RLCQ either. Hopefully, when you are reading this book, the world will be stable and life for you will be thriving. But always be honest with yourself, and whenever you score the RLCQ, if your life is filled with changes that are not included in it, heed the warning signs of an *underestimated* LCU score.

Dunham and Varma (1998) cite research studies of teachers with high levels of *life stress*. Teachers with the most ongoing life stressors had their immune systems compromised, as measured by reduced T cells and natural killer cells in their blood, suggesting major reductions in their defense against infections. This would explain the Holmes and Rahe (1967a, 1967b) original predictions of illness onset because of chronic life stressors.

Good News!

Even if your LCU points are very high, you can delay many future life changes to ease the burden on you and your family.

If you have had too much change on your plate in the last year, delay new changes that you can control for at least six months, such as beginning a new class after work.

By now, you've taken the questionnaire, scored it, and may be feeling overwhelmed or hopeless, right? You're bracing yourself for what you believe is the inevitable onset of an illness or accident. But **hold the presses**! Remember the questions I posed in the preface? Are some people just better suited to deal with stress than others? How can some teachers thrive under the same stressful circumstances and events under which others collapse? Is there a stress-prone personality type that makes some teachers more vulnerable to these stressors? Can we learn how to increase the effectiveness of how we cope with the stressors that surround us? These questions all have answers that can help you to feel optimistic about your life, despite your score.

THE LIFE EVENT STRESSORS INHERENT IN TEACHING

I have never worked in a coalmine, or a uranium mine, or in a herring trawler; but I know from experience that working in a bank from 9:15 to 5:30, and once in four weeks the whole of Saturday, with two weeks holidays a year, was a rest cure compared to teaching in a school.

—T. S. Eliot, poet

Obviously, teachers not only have to deal with all of the life events changes that are delineated in the RLCQ and all of the stressors they are enduring in their nation and world, but also they have a whole host of additional stressors to deal with every day. Second-grade teacher Mary C., who was named a Milken National Educator, admits that sometimes her job can be overwhelming: "We all think we know what school is about because we all went to school, What you can't know is the decision making that goes on in a teacher's head—it's a lot of thinking on your feet" (Wolfe, 2008, p. 3).

Table 2.2 is a checklist of some potential job stressors in teaching. The stressors are categorized to help you logically examine the specific challenges

Table 2.2   Checklist of Potential Job Stressors by Category

Check all that apply to you, and add others that are not on the list.	
Important/Changeable	*Unimportant/Changeable*
❏ Addressing needs of diverse-skilled students ❏ Addressing new student needs ❏ Balancing conflicting time demands from your family ❏ Balancing time demands ❏ Classroom management and disruption issues ❏ Dealing with an irate coworker ❏ Fear of violence ❏ Feeling that whatever you do doesn't matter to the students ❏ Grading homework and tests ❏ Having bus duty added ❏ Having communication difficulties with parents, administrators, and/or colleagues ❏ Having little input in decision making related to your role	*❏ Time crunch in running errands before going home* *❏ Volunteering to take on extra projects* *❏ Work you prefer to complete in school before going home* ❏ ❏ ❏

(Continued)

Table 2.2   (Continued)

Important/Changeable	Unimportant/Changeable
❏ Isolation from other adults for most of the day ❏ Learning new technology ❏ Maintaining classroom order ❏ Making new lesson plans ❏ Managing excessive paperwork ❏ Mastering new subject matter ❏ Multiple role demands (social worker, guidance counselor, nurse, babysitter, attorney, lunchtime supervisor, fundraiser, and parental doormat) ❏ Parent conferences ❏ ❏ ❏	❏ ❏ ❏
Important/Unchangeable	*Unimportant/Unchangeable*
❏ Accountability demands ❏ Constant assessments ❏ Demanding legislative/governmental programs ❏ Hurricane or other natural disaster in your school community ❏ Monitoring restraining orders ❏ Monitoring student medications ❏ Overcrowded classroom ❏ Poor parental cooperation ❏ Stretched budgets, fewer assistants ❏ Sudden illness keeping you out of the classroom for several days ❏ Teaching students at different levels of interest, skill, and background ❏ Threat of lawsuit ❏ Working for a nasty or uncooperative principal ❏ ❏ ❏	❏ *Bad weather* ❏ *Spilled food on clothes during lunch* ❏ *Traffic to and from school* ❏ ❏ ❏

that you face at your job. You can view your potential stressors in the following categories: important/changeable, important/unchangeable, unimportant/changeable, and unimportant/unchangeable. I have filled in many potential stressors for you. Simply check off the ones you have to deal with and add ones that apply to you that are not included in the table. Be careful to put the new ones in the correct box, according to importance and changeability.

What is important here is your perception of the importance and changeability of each stressor. The more stressors you see as changeable, the more control you will feel. Frequently, we see stressors as out of our control when they really are not. Some creative thinking and brainstorming (alone and with your teaching colleagues) can go a long way toward recognizing that you have more control than you thought.

Now, before you get overwhelmed by all of this and contemplate turning in your resignation, there is help on the way!

The United States Department of Education (DEA) statistics for the school year 2003–2004 showed that 8.4% of the nation's public school teachers quit their jobs during that year, and 56% of them said they did so because they were unhappy with teaching (Parker-Pope, 2008). Furthermore, confirming the statistics noted in the preface, the DEA also admitted that close to a third of new teachers leave the profession after just three years, and nearly a half leave after five years (Parker-Pope)!

But that leaves many teachers *not* quitting, despite enduring the same stressors. Why is it that not all teachers exposed to similar stress-provoking situations experi-

> # Good News!
>
> As you can see in Table 2.3 (page 30), each chapter of this book is filled with practical, how-to methods of preventing or modifying your stress, regardless of its source. This table is your handy reference guide to examine coping prescriptions for virtually any job stressor that exists. Put a paper clip on this page so you can go back to it quickly whenever you need to.

ence the same degree of stress? Just like the story of Debbie in Chapter 1, examples of success stories will be revealed in each subsequent chapter.

Remember Connie B.? She had several unchangeable events take place in her life in a short period, including the death of her mother and her husband divorcing her. These events happened just when she began a master's program in the evenings. Feeling overwhelmed, she contemplated quitting her teaching job.

Connie recognized that making additional changes after the ones that she went through in the past six months would only increase her stress, so she decided to keep her job and stay in her master's program. She began to examine her negative thinking, which was causing her depression and overwhelmed feelings. She used the Thinking-Pattern Worksheet (TPW) and the Thought-Stopping Technique (both coming up in Chapter 5) to change her whole outlook.

Table 2.3   Checklist of Coping Prescriptions by Stressor Category

Check each prescription you review and use.	
Important/Changeable	*Unimportant/Changeable*
These types of job stressors are addressed best by assertively taking charge of each situation and making necessary changes, thus reducing stress. ❏ Bring issues up in staff meetings ❏ Develop time-management skills (see Chapter 4) ❏ Maintain social support (see Chapter 8) ❏ Use active-listening skills with students, spouse and colleagues (see Chapter 4) ❏ Use assertiveness skills (see Chapter 4) ❏ ❏ ❏	*Because these potential stressors are perceived by you to be relatively unimportant, just try to disregard them and let them go. If you find you can readjust these situations, go ahead and do it because you will feel better and perhaps it will build your confidence.* *All of the same skills described in the boxes to the left will work for these potential stressors, as well.*
Important/Unchangeable	*Unimportant/Unchangeable*
These job stressors are the most difficult to deal with because they are important, but you have no obvious way to control them. Left alone, these stressors can be overwhelming, lead to burnout, and feelings of hopelessness and helplessness. But you certainly can do many things to help yourself, including changing the way you think about situations that you can't change: ❏ Balance your life. (See Chapter 4) ❏ Bring humor into your life. (See Chapter 7) ❏ Focus on the positive aspects of your life. (See Chapter 3)	*Since you view these potential stressors as unimportant, don't even bother with them.* *Everybody has these unpredictable hassles. Just go with the flow here and give yourself permission to ignore them.* *If you really must deal with these, you can certainly use the same prescriptions described in the boxes to the left.*

Important/Unchangeable	Unimportant/Unchangeable
❏ Give yourself a "worry time." (If you must worry, each day allow yourself a maximum of 10 minutes to worry and always do it at the same time. Save all of your worrying for this time and do not allow yourself to worry for the rest of the day. Once your worry time is over for the day, focus on positive thinking.)	
❏ Maintain social support in and out of school. (See Chapter 8)	
❏ Practice relaxation techniques. (See Resource C)	
❏ Practice stress-hardiness techniques. (See Chapter 6)	
❏ Recognize your *negative thinking* and *distorted thoughts*. It's fine to pay attention to the stressors you cannot change and come up with creative plans to deal with them, but it is completely overreacting to think doom and gloom, catastrophic thoughts. The result will be that you will change your emotional reactions to these stressors. (See Chapter 3)	
❏ Set goals and action plans for the future so you feel more in control. (See Chapter 6)	
❏ Use the Thinking-Pattern Worksheet (TPW) (See Chapter 5)	
❏ Use the Thought-Stopping Technique (See Chapter 5)	
❏	
❏	
❏	

┌─ **Good News!** ──────────────┐

Events in your life represent only about 10% of your stress. What you do about those events—particularly what you say to yourself about those events—represents the other 90%. Guess what? You can learn to control what you say to yourself about any event that befalls you. So smile and take a deep breath. Chapter 3 will teach you exactly how to do this.

└──────────────────────────────┘

Connie realized that her husband's behavior before he left her was abusive and that she was dependent on him in a very unhealthy way. Ultimately, she recognized that she was much better without him in her life. While she mourned the death of her mother, she focused much of her spare time on her father and sister, building a support base with them. Her focus on teaching picked up quickly and in eight months, she had finished her master's degree and was feeling much better.

Let go of resentment you are harboring toward anyone or anything. Don't harbor grudges. Forgive those who have hurt you and move on.

For the next two weeks, keep a pad next to your bed. Each night, reflect on the day's activities and events. Write, on separate lines, at least five things you are grateful for that occurred during the last 24 hours.

ACTION PLAN FOR STRESS MASTERY

Table 2.4	My Action Plan for Stress Mastery

Check off when completed.	
New Behavior	*What I Did and the Date Accomplished*
☐ I will mark my calendar to fill out the Recent Life Changes Questionnaire (RLCQ) every six months and total my points. ☐ ☐ ☐	What I did: Date accomplished:

New Behavior	*What I Did and the Date Accomplished*
☐ If my points are too high for the last six months, I will delay making any major changes during the next six months. ☐ ☐ ☐	What I did: Date accomplished:
☐ I will categorize all of my job stressors into *important, unimportant, changeable,* and *unchangeable.* ☐ ☐ ☐	What I did: Date accomplished:
☐ I will look up the specific coping and preventive prescriptions to help me with each potential stressor I have. I will check off and practice at least one of those prescriptions daily. ☐ ☐ ☐	What I did: Date accomplished:

REFERENCES

Atkinson, W. (2004). *Eliminate stress from your life forever.* New York: Amacom.

Culligan, M. J., & Sedlacek, K. (1976). *How to avoid stress before it kills you.* New York: Gramercy.

Dunham, J., & Varma, V. (Eds.). (1998). *Stress in teachers: Past, present, and future.* London: Whurr.

Gold, Y., & Roth, R. (1993). *Teachers managing stress.* London: Falmer Press.

Hawkins, N. G., Davies, R., & Holmes, T. H. (1957). Evidence of psychosocial factors in the development of pulmonary tuberculosis. *American Review of Tuberculosis and Pulmonary Diseases, 75,* 768–780.

Holmes, T. H., & Masuda, M. (1970). *Life change and illness susceptibility.* Paper presented at the annual meeting of the American Association for the Advancement of Science, Chicago, IL.

Holmes, T. H., & Rahe, R. H. (1967a). *Schedule of recent experiences.* Seattle: University of Washington School of Medicine.

Holmes, T. H., & Rahe, R. H. (1967b). The social readjustment rating scale. *Journal of Psychosomatic Research, 11,* 213–218.

Miller, M., & Rahe, R. (1997). Life changing scaling for the 1990s. *Journal of Psychosomatic Research, 43,* 279–292.

Parker-Pope, T. (2008, January 2). *Teacher burnout? Blame the parents.* Retrieved April 11, 2009, from http://well.blogs.nytimes.com/2008/01/02/teacher-burnout-blame-the-parents/.

Seyle, H. (1976). *The stress of life.* New York: Ballantine Books.

Wolfe, F. S. (2008, Fall). *Mrs. Cowhey's classroom.* Retrieved April 11, 2009, from http://www.umassmag.com/2008/fall_2008/Features/index.html.

3

How to Recognize the Real Culprit: Your Internal Critic

All of us have collected thoughts and beliefs and ideas about ourselves that weigh us down and hold us back from reaching so many of the opportunities that life holds in store for us.

—Shad Helmstetter (1982)

LEARNING OBJECTIVES

- I will understand the origins of my beliefs and my *internal critic.*
- I will be able to explain the relationship between my thoughts, emotions, and behaviors.
- I will be able to examine my negative thoughts in the context of the 10 distorted self-talk patterns.
- Anytime I feel any negative emotion, I will be able to recognize the thoughts that led to that emotion, and then I will challenge those thoughts with nine key questions.
- Once I ask myself the nine key questions, I will use the A-B-C-D-E model to calm my emotions.
- I will make it a habit to focus my thinking on the things in life that I am grateful for and I am proud of.

Joel S. began his teaching career late in life. He was a practicing attorney when he decided that he'd missed his calling. Soon he found himself teaching civics and social studies at the high school level. Entering the classroom the first day, he was faced with more than 30 students with a range of skill and ability levels.

He found that if he assigned classwork or homework to accommodate the slower learners, the other students became bored. On the other hand, if he directed his assignments toward the higher achievers, the lesser-skilled students were lost. Predictably, he also discovered that teaching to the average student failed to reduce the numbers of those either frustrated or turned off.

Joel came home at night frustrated and feeling like a failure. He felt hopeless, and his teaching colleagues reinforced his conclusion that there was no solution to this problem. They told him to just do his best and not worry about losing some students along the way. He was so discouraged that he contemplated quitting teaching and drafting a resignation letter. So what happened to Joel? Stay tuned.

As I noted in Chapter 2, it has been estimated that about 10% of the stress people feel at any time results from recent events in their lives; but a hefty 90% of the stress results from their *internal dialogue* related to those events (Helmstetter, 1982, 1987). Your self-talk determines whether an event in your life will lead to stress. This internal dialogue is based on your thinking habits and patterns, and these specific patterns of thoughts determine the degree of stress any event will provoke.

THE ORIGINS OF OUR BELIEF SYSTEMS

We are influenced not by "facts" but by our interpretation of facts.

—Alfred Adler, colleague of Freud
and cofounder of the psychoanalytic movement

Our beliefs and self-talk about any event that takes place in our lives are based on our habitual ways of looking at similar situations. It all starts with the words and phrases we use when talking to ourselves—our *inner dialogue*.

All of us have a little voice in our heads that we listen to hundreds of times a day. (If you happen to have more than one voice, call your local mental health specialist right away.) Sadly, that voice inside our heads, more often than not, is filling our minds with negative, irrational, self-defeating statements, such as, "I'll never be able to do that," or "I'm a failure," and, "I don't see any way to change my situation."

Researcher and author Shad Helmstetter (1982, 1987), cites research that shows that at least 75% of everything we think about is negative, self-defeating, pessimistic, and counterproductive. So many of our thoughts are self-defeating, not necessarily true, or based on inaccurate information, yet we habitually fill our brains with scary, depressing, worrisome self-talk.

How did we develop these unfortunate thinking habits? The answer lies in fascinating research cited by Dr. Helmstetter (1982). By the time youngsters in the United States reach the age of 18, most have been negatively *programmed* with critical feedback, often by well-meaning parents, teachers, and other authority figures who believe they are helping those youngsters. Besides being told "No!" or what we cannot do, we receive much negative programming, such as, "You aren't pretty enough to be chosen for homecoming queen, so don't embarrass yourself by trying"; "You won't make the football team"; "Music is not a major that will help you in life, so don't waste your time"; "That's too risky, so don't attempt it"; "Don't worry, I don't expect you to do well anyway"; and "Why can't you be more like your sister?"

From my own experience, a misinformed high school guidance counselor once told my parents, "Jack is not college material, so you can save the money you would have spent on tuition and prepare him for a trade instead." Later, you'll learn how I turned those absurd comments from a "professional" into personal motivation.

Helmstetter (1982) claims that during the first 18 years of life, most of us have heard negatives from these people at least 148,000 times versus only a few thousand positive comments about what we can do or can accomplish in life. It's no wonder, then, that with this ratio of 148,000 negatives to 3,000 or 4,000 positives, most of us are programmed to think negatively, fear taking risks, have low self-confidence and self-esteem, and tend to be constantly critical of ourselves. In short, this is the beginning of the development of what I call our *internal critic*.

You might think that once we grow older, we are no longer under the influence of our early life programming, from our parents, teachers, and others who "care" about us. But sadly, most of us pick right up where that negative programming left off. In other words, we continue to beat ourselves up with the same negative, self-critical, distorted thoughts that were originally "planted" into our subconscious minds by others. As one of my cherished mentors, Dr. Lee Pulos (2004): put it,

> *The subconscious mind is like a garden full of beautiful flowers. Sadly, we have had weeds planted in that garden by well-meaning, but misinformed parents, teachers, siblings and other people with whom we interact . . . and then we continue to fertilize and water those weeds with our own habitual negative thoughts and beliefs. (Paper presented at a meeting of the American Society of Clinical Hypnosis, Denver, Colorado)*

As we continue to beat ourselves up with an internal dialogue of self-doubt, worry, fear, and lack of confidence, our belief systems, attitudes, and behaviors develop our *internal critic*. See Figure 3.1 for an illustration.

Figure 3.1   The Origins and Consequences of Our Internal Critic

- From our parents and other significant adults, we become programmed with negative, self-defeating ideas about ourselves, and as a result, our INTERNAL CRITIC is formed.
- We pick up where they left off and continue to fuel our internal critic with our own negative SELF-TALK.
- Our internal critic creates negative BELIEFS.
- Our beliefs create negative ATTITUDES.
- Our attitudes create negative FEELINGS, MOODS, and EMOTIONS.
- Our feelings, moods, and emotions create negative BEHAVIORS and even negatively impact our immune system.
- Our negative behaviors are self-fulfilling prophecies, and they fuel the negative, self-defeating thoughts that make up our internal critic, so this is a CONTINUOUS CIRCLE,

Unless we intervene in the process.

This cycle of negativity, beginning with the words from our parents, siblings, teachers, and others, establishes the foundation of our belief systems, attitudes, emotions, and behaviors, which is habitually reinforced in our minds, by us. So it's not the events, but our habitual, negative *internal interpretation* of those events, that ultimately leads to our stress.

Here's what we know about internal thoughts, our *self-talk.* Helmstetter (1987) reports that neuroscientists have proof that all "thoughts are electrical impulses that trigger electrical and chemical switches in the brain" (p. 14). Whenever a thought takes place, the brain releases chemicals to set off specific additional chemical, electrical, and physical responses in the body. If a thought is negative or frightening, these physical responses switch on the sympathetic nervous system (SNS), causing what Seyle (1976) called the stress-response syndrome to take place. If the thought is positive, encouraging, and optimistic, the parasympathetic nervous system is triggered, leading us to feel calm, confident, and happy.

It's important to understand that the brain always takes orders from us and simply records what it receives. It doesn't matter if the thought was based on reality, a lie, or a distortion of reality. As an example, if you close your eyes and imagine yourself lying on a beach in Hawaii, with the turquoise ocean in front of you, a gentle breeze coming off the water, feeling the rays of the sun warming your body, you can eventually feel a calming, very comfortable feeling come over you, as the thought triggers the parasympathetic nervous system. This type of visualizing is actually the basis for the power of hypnosis. Again, your subconscious mind doesn't know the difference between *actual* and *imagined* images or thoughts. It goes with whatever you put into it, good or bad, without judging it. As Helmstetter (1987) puts it, "Your subconscious mind will not care where that programming comes from or how it gets it. It will just continue to accept the input that is fed to it—right or wrong, for better or worse" (p. 18).

Repeating the same negative, self-critical thoughts to ourselves whenever we are in a similar situation develops a pattern of repeated, stress-causing reactions in our brains.

> *The brain makes no moral judgments; it simply accepts what you tell it. . . . It makes no difference whether the things you have told yourself or believed about yourself in the past were true or not.* The brain doesn't care! *(Helmstetter, 1982, p. 59)*

Self-talk habits develop connections in your subconscious mind between situations, your interpretation of those situations, and immediate chemical and electrical connections to the appropriate nervous system. So it's critical to understand and take charge of your self-talk habits.

Taking command of your self-talk, regardless of past programming from others and reinforcement from your thinking habits, can develop *new programming* in your subconscious mind. It is up to you. You really can change those thinking habits!

When my guidance counselor told my parents that I wasn't college material, I had two choices: I could have either accepted the opinion of this "expert," and therefore resigned myself to the "fact" that I didn't have what it takes to succeed in college or I could have stood at that crossroad in my life and told myself that he was dead wrong about me and I could prove it. Fortunately for me, I chose the second path.

Good News!

Repeating positive, healthy thoughts to yourself can permanently change the mental connections established by your old thinking habits.

Many years later, after earning a bachelor and master's degree, a PhD, a postdoctorate, and several individual honors, I returned to my high school to display my diplomas to that counselor. I told him that he needs to be careful what he says to students and their families. His words certainly could have destroyed my future, and they may very well have destroyed others, who simply gave up.

Table 3.1 gives examples of self-talk that provoke negative emotions and stress. Many of these thoughts could have originated with comments from your parents, for example, and then were reinforced by you restating those thoughts hundreds of times to yourself over the years. Are you a victim of any of these self-talk examples?

Table 3.1	Examples of Stress-Provoking, Distorted Self-Talk

> "I'm not as good as the other teachers in my school."
>
> "My future as a teacher looks bleak."
>
> "Everything I do turns out badly."
>
> "I feel so much resentment, envy, fear, and sadness."
>
> "I am feeling hopeless."
>
> "I have no control over my destiny."
>
> "No one can help me feel better."
>
> "No one really cares about me the way I need them to."
>
> "I've always failed, and this is another example."
>
> "I'm stupid, and I'll never figure out what to do about my situation."

OUR SELF-TALK AND OUR EMOTIONS

There's nothing either good or bad but thinking makes it so.

—William Shakespeare, *Hamlet*

As you now understand, stress is *not* about what happens to you. Stress results from what you *say to yourself* about what happens to you. You can choose to think in a healthy fashion, regardless of what kinds of thoughts you have allowed to enter your subconscious mind, unchallenged, in the past. William James, famous American philosopher and psychologist, said it best: "The greatest weapon against stress is our ability to choose one thought over another" (2009).

Good News!

You always choose what to say to yourself about any event or situation in which you find yourself. Since the choice is yours, give yourself healthy, calming thoughts.

Let's revisit the unhealthy, stress-provoking examples in Table 3.1 and replace them with the rational, optimistic, self-talk examples in Table 3.2.

Table 3.2	Examples of Healthy, Rational Self-Talk

"I have special skills that make me a real asset as a teacher."

"My future as a teacher looks great. I don't have to be perfect to be a fine teacher."

"I make mistakes like everyone else, but I learn from my mistakes."

"I experience negative emotions, but I find ways to release them quickly and move on."

"No matter what happens in my life, I will remain optimistic that new opportunities for happiness are just around the corner."

"I control the thoughts in my mind, and I choose to stop negative thoughts quickly and replace them with positive ones."

"I am ultimately responsible for the way I feel because I am in control of my thinking. I choose to forgive others and to forgive myself for mistakes I have made."

"Right now, I may have no one special in my life, but I will hold positive images and goals in my mind, as well as pictures of what I truly want. I am confident that sooner or later, special, caring people will enter my life, and I will be very happy."

"When I have failed in the past, it has been because of my negative programming. I now know how to move beyond those thoughts and to be successful. It just takes practice and consistency."

"I'm smart enough to realize where my thinking has caused my problems in the past and what I need to do to change those habits."

Recognize that you are not a prisoner of past programming. Just because you heard negative comments from your parents and others does not make those statements accurate. You can choose to disregard them, and you can decide not to repeat them to yourself. Instead, repeat healthy, optimistic thoughts to yourself daily.

It's reasonable to assume that there is a direct cause-and-effect relationship between an event or situation people find themselves in and their emotional reactions to that event. For example, recall our high school civics and social studies teacher, Joel. He found himself with 30 students in his class possessing the whole spectrum of ability levels and wondering how to make his class interesting, motivating, and educational for all of these students. The situation (or event) he faced was a classroom full of students he needed to teach, with a mixture of slow learners and high achievers. He came home at night feeling hopeless and helpless. Using information from Figure 3.2, one might assume that the classroom situation was the activating event (A) that caused Joel to feel the stressful emotions of hopelessness and helplessness (C1), and those feelings led to the stressful behavioral reaction of considering quitting his profession (C2).

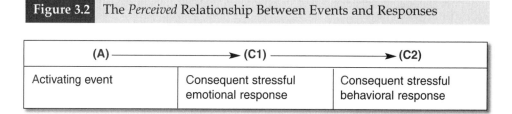

Figure 3.2   The *Perceived* Relationship Between Events and Responses

(A) ───────────► (C1) ───────────► (C2)		
Activating event	Consequent stressful emotional response	Consequent stressful behavioral response

Because of a tremendous volume of research in the area of Cognitive/ Behavioral Therapy, much of which is found in Dr. David Burns's book, *The Feeling Good Handbook* (1989), it has now been well established that your *thoughts, beliefs, and attitudes—not* the events and situations in which you find yourself—create and cause your emotional reactions and your resultant behavioral responses. This relationship can be understood best using the **A-B-C** model in Figure 3.3.

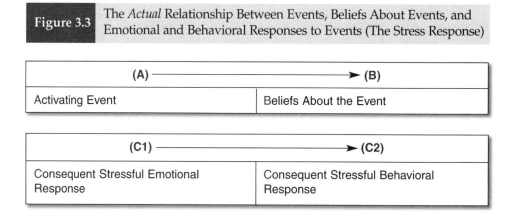

Figure 3.3   The *Actual* Relationship Between Events, Beliefs About Events, and Emotional and Behavioral Responses to Events (The Stress Response)

(A) ───────────────────► (B)	
Activating Event	Beliefs About the Event

(C1) ───────────────────► (C2)	
Consequent Stressful Emotional Response	Consequent Stressful Behavioral Response

As you can see, it's *not* the activating event (A), per se, that produces the consequent emotions and behaviors (C1, C2), but it is *your belief about* or *interpretation of that event* (B) that causes the consequent emotional (C1) and behavioral (C2) reactions.

You can easily remember this process using the equation in Figure 3.4.

| Figure 3.4 | Simplified Equation of the Stress Response Relationship |

$$(A) + (B) = (C1) + (C2)$$

Any event plus your beliefs about the event leads to your emotional and behavioral reactions to that event.

So when Joel learned about the range of ability levels in his class **(A)**, he immediately began to think about himself and the situation at hand in a negative, pessimistic way **(B)**. He began to tell himself that he would make a mistake and some of the students would go home complaining to their parents. It was these *thoughts* that caused him to feel stressed **(C1)**. After consulting with his pessimistic colleagues, these thoughts were reinforced and, ultimately, his emotions reached a level where he thought that his only relief from the situation would come from writing a resignation letter to his principal **(C2)**.

Clearly, Joel's negative thoughts about his situation and his inner dialogue led to his emotional and behavioral reactions. Those reactions were *not* simply the result of the class situation (event) itself. Joel had choices as to what to say to himself about the situation. As examples, here are some alternative thoughts Joel could have given himself:

I have been in difficult dilemmas before and found creative ways to solve them. I cannot please everyone, so I will teach to the average ability level in my class and offer those who may have difficulty extra time after school. I have been told by students in the past that I am a wonderful teacher and I know that I will make many of my students happy with my teaching style. I don't have to please every single student to consider myself a success.

The next time you feel any negative emotion (overwhelmed, depressed, irritated, impatient, or hopeless), list the specific thoughts that went through your mind just before you felt that emotion. This is the first step in recovering from your stress.

EXPOSE AND DISPOSE OF YOUR INTERNAL CRITIC

If you are pained by an external thing, it is not this external thing that disturbs you, but your own judgment about it. And it is in your own power to wipe out this judgment now.

—Marcus Aurelius, philosopher

To challenge our internal critic and render it impotent, we need to understand our distorted-thinking patterns and the alternative thoughts that we have available to us. As I pointed out earlier, the "weeds" that were planted in our subconscious minds by our parents and other authority figures were then "watered and fertilized" by us, as we perpetuated those unfortunate thinking habits.

Common Negative Self-Talk Patterns

If you want to break out of a bad mood, you must first understand that every type of negative feeling results from a specific kind of negative thought.

—Dr. David Burns (1989)

We now know that our internal critic consists of persistent patterns of negative, self-defeating thoughts that we quickly employ when we encounter difficult situations or events. Learning about these unfortunate, distorted-thinking patterns is the first step in making life-altering changes in our thinking. The definitions of these patterns are based on the pioneering work by Dr. Matt McKay (1981) and Dr. David Burns (1989). Ten common negative-thinking patterns are found in Table 3.3. Copy the table and keep it handy for quick reference.

Table 3.3 Ten Negative Self-Talk Patterns

Self-Talk Pattern	Example of Internal Dialogue (Check off if you believe you are thinking this way)
☐ *All or nothing*	*"If I can't motivate every one of my students, regardless of ability level, I have failed."*
☐ *Magnification*	*"It would be really awful if any of my students didn't like me."*
☐ *Mind reading*	*"If my colleague is irritated, it must be because of something I've done or said."*
☐ *Catastrophizing or fortune-telling*	*"What if my principal asked to see me because he is going to fire me? What will I do? My husband will be so upset with me."*
☐ *Having to be right*	*"I don't care what the rules say. If I have a disruptive child in my class, I have the right to embarrass him or her in front of the entire class."*

☐ *I should, I must, I have to*	*"I should be able handle the multiple roles of teacher, counselor, nurse, attorney, and doormat for parents. That's my job."*
☐ *Mental filter*	*"I don't care how many parents praise me. Even if only one criticizes me, I can't get that out of my mind. I am a failure."*
☐ *Overgeneralization*	*"I always have trouble on standardized tests, so I will probably fail the proficiency test I have to take."*
☐ *Blaming*	*"My poor evaluation was only because the principal doesn't like me."*
☐ *Emotional reasoning*	*"How could I make the same mistake twice? I really must be stupid."*

All-or-Nothing Thinking

With this distorted thinking, you look at your world as strictly black or white, good or bad. Such thinking often involves attempting to be perfect, which is obviously impossible. You believe if you can't do something perfectly, then you have failed.

A teacher forgets to give all of the information necessary to complete the homework problems she assigns. When she gets home, she realizes the error, asks herself, "How can I call myself a good math teacher when I didn't even give them the information they need to solve the problems?"

Magnification

In this distortion, you take things out of perspective and dramatically intensify what is actually happening. You use dramatic words, like *awful, disgusting,* and *terrible* to describe situations and outcomes that are rarely that critical.

This magnification of what is actually happening leads to scenarios such as the following: A teacher has to deal with a messy custody situation and must decide whether to release a child to her father after school. The teacher has a court order permitting such a release, but the mother has pleaded with the teacher to call her immediately if the father shows up because she does not want her daughter going home with the father during the school week. The teacher thinks, "If I do the wrong thing here, it will be awful."

The reality is that a mistake here may be unfortunate and could even lead to a parent complaining to the principal, but it's unlikely that the situation would be *terrible* or really *awful*—terms that should be reserved for really bad situations, like natural disasters or losing one's job. We call this tendency to magnify *awfulizing*.

Mind Reading

This is a very common pattern. You conclude that somehow you have an ESP-like understanding of what people are feeling and thinking about you. Often, you conclude that people whom you know "are thinking or feeling something negative about me," even though you have no real evidence to support this conclusion—you just "feel" it, so you believe it to be true.

A teacher is sent a note stating that the principal would like to speak to her during the lunch break. The teacher reads the note and immediately concludes: "What did I do wrong? I must be in some kind of trouble here."

Catastrophizing or Fortune-Telling

The tip-off to this pattern is the use of "what ifs." You take a situation or event and blow it out of proportion by *assuming* that a disastrous outcome is on its way. You come to expect a catastrophic conclusion, as if you have a crystal ball to look into the future and (of course) you usually expect that outcome to be something negative.

In the previous example, the teacher not only assumes that the principal is angry with her, but she starts to worry about being fired. "Oh my gosh, what if my principal is calling me in to fire me? How will I tell my husband? And what about our family? How can we support them when I lose my job? Will we need to go on welfare? And how will this look to my parents and our friends?"

You can imagine how such catastrophic thoughts can easily lead to the emotions of despair, hopelessness, and fear. The result, in terms of behavior, could be avoidance of the fear-producing situation, such as avoiding speaking with the principal by finding reasons to leave school during lunch breaks and at the end of the school day. The teacher might even begin to develop vague physical symptoms, leading to increased absences—all psychologically to avoid the principal.

Having to Be Right

Having to be right all of the time develops out of insecurity. This is based on a fear related to worrying about what it says about you if you are wrong. Therefore, you don't listen to another person's point of view or logic that may prove your position on an issue to be wrong. After all, you don't know how to deal with being wrong.

A teacher feels threatened by suggestions that he is not updating his lesson plan. Consequently, he ignores the suggestions of his colleagues and, fearing blame, stubbornly persists, continually justifying the outdated lesson plan.

I Should, I Must, and I Have To

People who frequently use words like these in their thinking are making an unconscious assumption that there is a universal list of ironclad rules (besides the laws of the land and your particular religious commandments) to which we must all adhere. If you break the rule ("I shouldn't have done that."), it leads to feelings of guilt. If someone else breaks the rule ("She should have done this."), it results in you feeling frustrated or angry.

Although we often regret actions that had unfortunate outcomes, and we may use the word *should* on ourselves, the *continual* use of such words leaves no room for innocent mistakes. There is no room here to give yourself a break.

Prior to handing out a peanut snack to her students, a teacher forgets to check to see if any student is allergic to peanuts. A student has a reaction, and even though such a reaction could be serious, the teacher cannot forgive her memory lapse. Instead, she beats herself up unmercifully with self-talk like, "I should have been more careful. I could have killed that student. I am incompetent and shouldn't be teaching."

Mental Filter

This form of distorted thinking involves having tunnel vision when it comes to positives in your life. You can have 10 positive things happen, but you dwell only on the single negative experience you had.

A teacher gets a very good performance review from her principal, but there is a single comment suggesting a behavior that the principal says could use some improvement. Instead of focusing on the positive feedback, the teacher comes away from the meeting highly upset. She can't stop thinking thoughts, such as the following: "I have failed, and my principal is upset with me." (This is also mind reading.)

Overgeneralization

You have an unfortunate incident, and you believe that is the beginning of a never-ending pattern of similar episodes. The tip-off to this kind of thinking is the frequent use of words such as *never, always, all, every, and none*. These absolutes are exaggerations of reality, and they are extremely self-defeating.

A teacher is told that he will have to take a proficiency test and because he once struggled with a test at the end of college, he tells himself, "I always have trouble on these kinds of tests, and I won't be able to pass it." (This is also fortune-telling.)

Blaming

This in an interesting example of distorted thinking because there is some fascinating research suggesting that you may actually want to find someone or something to blame when you fail to accomplish something important to you. As you will discover in Chapter 8, there are often decided advantages to finding an excuse to explain failure rather than blaming yourself, as if you are incompetent. The real problem with blaming, however, is when you *constantly* berate yourself for every unhappy or unfortunate situation that befalls you or you rarely take responsibility and quickly blame others for your misfortunes.

A teacher gets a poor evaluation from the principal and rationalizes that the principal has it in for her, rather than accepting the criticism and understanding that this feedback will help her to become a better teacher.

Emotional Reasoning

This example of distorted thinking involves drawing the wrong conclusion based on your emotions at the time. Because you feel an emotion or have a thought, you conclude that it must be true. For example, if you make a mistake and *feel* stupid, you conclude, "I must be stupid." If you feel anger, you conclude that the person in question must have done something bad to you, rather than realize that your angry emotions may be based on faulty thinking or not having all of the information.

A teacher is reprimanded by his principal for missing a faculty meeting. The teacher actually was dealing with a family crisis and completely forgot the meeting, yet when he was reprimanded, he felt like a child being scolded for being bad. He then concludes something to the effect that he must be immature and deserves to be reprimanded.

 Recognize the specific negative self-talk patterns you have developed. Make a list of common negative thoughts you have in a typical day and check the list of 10 common distorted-thinking patterns to determine which ones you engage in regularly.

The most important part of the process of eliminating the emotional, physical, and behavioral consequences of adverse events that take place in our lives is recognizing the distortions in our thinking and beliefs about those events. The next step is challenging, or *disputing* those thoughts. You don't have to believe your negative and scary thoughts. Thoughts lie; they can mislead you, tease you, and frighten you. Just because they cross your mind doesn't make them true.

There are several key questions you can ask yourself regarding each thought that you are aware of, which may belong to a negative-thinking pattern. Copy Table 3.4 so you will have these key questions for quick reference to challenge your negative thoughts.

Table 3.4	Quick Reference Guide of Questions to Challenge Your Negative Thinking

- "What negative situation am I assuming is (or will be) happening to me?"
- "What is the evidence to support my conclusions?"
- "Could I be exaggerating the situation in my mind?"
- "Am I turning a minor setback into a major catastrophe in my mind?"
- "Is there any alternative explanation that could explain what happened or what will happen next? Could I be confusing facts with reoccurring thoughts in my mind?"
- "Are my conclusions based on emotions rather than on facts?"
- "Can I really predict the future?"
- "Am I using extreme words and phrases in my thoughts?"
- "Am I assuming the worst will happen without evidence of that?"

- "What negative situation am I assuming is (or will be) happening to me?"

  Try to identify the specific situation, event, or concern that triggered your negative thoughts in the first place. It's usually about bad things that have happened in the past or frightening things that you believe will take place in the future.

- "What is the evidence to support my conclusions?"

  If you are a beginning teacher and you conclude after one month that you will never be successful, where is the evidence to support that belief? Can you be 100% certain of this conclusion? Perhaps you haven't been successful (whatever that constitutes in your mind) up until now, but by learning from and brainstorming with your colleagues, you may very well learn the tricks of the trade to be quite successful down the road.

- "Could I be exaggerating the situation in my mind?"

  Perfectionistic thinkers tend to talk to themselves in terms of certainties. "The principal looks upset. She must be angry with me." You react as if there is 100% certainty of your conclusion from the principal's expressions or behavior. If you ask yourself what the probability is that she is mad at you based on all of the information you have, you'll be surprised how quickly you can dismiss what you earlier concluded was a certainty. Most of us tend to exaggerate the inevitability of bad outcomes and minimize the chances of good outcomes resulting from the situation we're in.

- "Am I turning a minor setback into a major catastrophe in my mind?"

  Everyone has unfortunate things that happen to them in their lives. Moreover, life is unpredictable, and you never know when these things will happen. A teacher has to deal with a disgruntled parent who says offensive things to the teacher during a parent-teacher conference. This does not mean any more than that parent has an issue with events that affected their youngster. Don't take that specific situation and the comments the parent made to you, which could be more a reflection of the issues that parent has in general, and blow it out of proportion, put yourself down, and/or decide that your skills are lacking.

- "Is there any alternative explanation that could explain what happened or what will happen next? Could I be confusing facts with reoccurring thoughts in my mind?"

  Often, we *assume* that something is true because we keep thinking about it in the same way. For example, if you frequently believe that your principal doesn't like you, you may believe it because you habitually think that way, but you probably don't have facts to prove whether your perception is accurate. Remember, your thoughts are not always based on facts but more on emotions, and we tend to habitually repeat the same thoughts to ourselves unless we recognize that they are distorted or not based on facts. Your thoughts are frequently the result of fears or fantasies and not based on the facts of the situation.

- "Are my conclusions actually based on my emotions rather than on facts?"

  The danger here is observing your feelings and emotions and concluding that they validate your thoughts. "Because I am nervous and frightened every time the principal observes my class, there must be something I'm doing wrong and I have reason to be afraid. So because I am afraid of what she will see, I'm sure that she's looking for grounds to fire me." This kind of thinking can lead to performance anxiety every time the principal enters your class to observe; thus, you have a self-fulfilling prophecy, which reinforces this vicious cycle of anxiety-producing thinking and the resultant frightening feelings.

- "Can I really predict the future?"

  Just because something unfortunate happened when you were in this situation before doesn't mean it is guaranteed to happen again.

Think about all of the other possible outcomes that could take place next time.

- "Am I using extreme words and phrases in my thoughts?"

  As I mentioned earlier, people often think in extremes and use terms such as *always, forever, never, should,* and *must* when they describe the way they see things. It's important to recognize when you are thinking this way and replace those words in your mind to words like *often* and *sometimes.*

- "Am I assuming the worst will happen without evidence to support that assumption?"

  Few situations are black or white, and you are not either perfect or a failure. Look at your situation without imagining extremes or thinking about the very worst thing that could happen, as if it is guaranteed to happen just because it crossed your mind.

Once you answer these key questions for yourself, you are on your way to exploring the specific distorted-thinking patterns that you may be using. Then, when you recognize the habitual, distorted-thinking pattern habits you use, you can develop rational rebuttals or disputes of your original thinking.

Whenever you recognize that you are upset and thinking negatively, use the quick reference guide of questions to challenge that negative thinking.

| Figure 3.5 | The A-B-C-D-E Model |

(A) ⟶	(B) ⟶	(C) ⟶	(D) ⟶	(E)
Activating event (stress)	Beliefs (thoughts) about the event	Consequent emotions and behaviors	Disputing thoughts	Energized, revitalized emotions

The **A-B-C** model now becomes the **A-B-C-D-E** model (Figure 3.5). Once we recognize the distortions in our beliefs and thoughts, we can *dispute* or challenge those beliefs and thoughts **(D)**, which then greatly diminishes the consequences **(C)** that arose before you realized your thinking was distorted. The result is positive, energized, and revitalized emotions **(E)**. In Chapter 5, you will find a convenient form, the

Thinking-Pattern Worksheet (TPW), which is a handy way of recognizing distorted thought patterns and disputing them.

Are you wondering whatever happened to our high school civics and social studies teacher, Joel S.? He was feeling helpless and didn't know how to effectively teach students with such a wide range of ability in the same class. But Joel was keenly aware of the fact that he had choices and was not a prisoner of his past negative thinking. After all, he did leave a thriving law practice to embrace his passion for teaching, so he already knew that he is was a risk taker, rather than someone feeling trapped in an occupation for an entire career.

Joel also realized he was overreacting and catastrophizing when he was feeling inadequate as a teacher. So he brainstormed, and came up with a practical idea. He decided to allow all of his students to choose their own modality in which to engage, work with, and learn the assigned material. Because each of them would be choosing to work in specific ways they enjoyed, Joel reasoned that they would be much more likely to (1) work more efficiently, (2) retain information and concepts longer and with more depth of understanding, and (3) be less disruptive or complain about Joel teaching to specific ability levels.

This idea worked like a charm. For example, if they were studying a historical event or era, the students could choose a traditional assignment, or as an alternative, they could choose to satisfy the assignment by creating one of the following:

1. A newspaper article,

2. A comic strip,

3. A play,

4. A song,

5. A poem,

6. A video,

7. A board game,

8. A report based on eyewitness report,

9. A report after a museum visit, or

10. Any other student-determined project that melds sufficient student involvement with the subject matter.

Joel became one of most beloved teachers at his school.

ACTION PLAN FOR STRESS MASTERY

Table 3.5   Action Plan for Stress Mastery

Check off when completed.	
New Behavior	*What I Did and the Date Accomplished*
❏ Every day I will remember that I have choices regarding how I think about myself and my life. I can choose to disregard the negative comments about me that my parents and others said. ❏ ❏ ❏	What I did: Date accomplished:
❏ I choose not to repeat those negative comments to myself. ❏ ❏ ❏	What I did: Date accomplished:
❏ Anytime I feel any negative emotion (overwhelmed, depressed, irritated, impatient, or hopeless), I will list the specific thoughts that preceded that emotion and use the A-B-C-D-E model to calm my emotions down. ❏ ❏ ❏	What I did: Date accomplished:

(Continued)

Table 3.5 (Continued)

❒ I will make a list of common negative thoughts that I have in a typical day and check the list of 10 common distorted thinking patterns to determine which ones I engage in regularly. ❒ ❒ ❒	What I did: Date accomplished:
❒ I will challenge my distorted thoughts by using the nine key questions found in this chapter. ❒ ❒ ❒	What I did: Date accomplished:
❒ I will make a list of the things in my life that I am grateful for, pin that list above my computer, or on my refrigerator, and look at it and add to it each day. ❒ ❒ ❒	What I did: Date accomplished:

REFERENCES

Burns, D. (1989). *The feeling good handbook.* New York: William Morrow.

Helmstetter, S. (1982). *What to say when you talk to yourself.* New York: Pocket Books.

Helmstetter, S. (1987). *The self-talk solution.* New York: Pocket Books.

James, William. (ND). Quote. ThinkExist.com. Retrieved September 29, 2009 from http://thinkexist.com/quotation/the_greatest_weapon_against_stress_is_our_ability/330010.html

McKay, M. D. (1981). *Thoughts & feelings.* Oakland, CA: New Harbinger.

Pulos, L. (2004, March). *Sports psychology and performance enhancement.* Paper presented at a meeting of the American Society of Clinical Hypnosis, Denver, CO.

Seyle, H. (1976). *The stress of life.* New York: Ballantine Books.

Singer, J. N. (1995). Conquering your internal critic so you can sing your own song. In D. M. Walters (Ed.), *Great speakers anthology* (Vol. 4, pp. 160–195). Glendora, CA: Royal.

4

How to Thrive Despite
Being Genetically Wired
With Stress-Prone
Personality Traits

We know now beyond any doubt what we suspected before—that Type-A behavior can be treated effectively.

—Meyer Friedman and Diane Ulmer (1984)

LEARNING OBJECTIVES

- I will determine whether I exhibit any of the Type-A behaviors, and if so, I will choose those behaviors I wish to modify and use the steps discussed in this chapter to help me to modify those behaviors.
- I will determine whether I exhibit any of the people-pleasing behaviors, and if so, I will use the steps discussed in this chapter to modify those behaviors.
- I will learn how to determine what situations provoke or trigger anger in me.
- I will learn how to use disputing self-talk to help reduce my anger and stress.
- I will learn how to eliminate free-floating hostility.
- I will practice assertive (not aggressive or nonassertive) behaviors.

Cheryl M. is a high school teacher. She has always been on the anxious side, both in and out of school. She is impatient in lines and in congested traffic, and she frequently gets so frustrated that she can feel her tension escalate. Speaking rapidly, she finds herself finishing sentences for people because they are just too slow for her.

For most of her life, she has found herself thinking about two or more things at the same time, and she thrives on multitasking. While on the phone, she often pretends to be listening while she is shuffling through her mail or clicking responses to e-mail on her computer. Because she considers wasting time almost a sin, she brushes her teeth while showering and always brings papers to grade or lesson plans she is working on with her to the restroom. Relaxation is foreign to her. She considers it a waste of time and believes that if she does take time just for herself, she will fail to accomplish her goals (recall the all-or-nothing thinking pattern). Because she puts the rest of her life on the back burner, doing things just for her is not a priority.

She has lofty goals, including being honored with the Teacher-of-the-Year award in her school, and she will do whatever it takes to accomplish this. Although her struggle to attain perfection in her career makes her a talented teacher, her competitive nature fuels free-floating hostility, which she doesn't realize she has. Her hostility comes to the surface when anyone or anything gets in the way of what she is trying to accomplish. Colleagues at her school accuse her of making "20 dollar reactions to 20 cent provocations." She is abrasive and downright rude when she is stressed.

Cheryl has a pervasive need to be in control of everything that she can in her life, including her classroom. Therefore, when a student speaks out of turn, Cheryl views this as a challenge to her need to be in control. Her impulsive reactions in such circumstances have resulted in several parents complaining to the principal that Cheryl has raised her voice at their children for relatively minor infractions. She has also used sarcasm and inappropriate humor, both of which were at the expense of her colleagues during staff meetings. You can see how Cheryl's teaching success comes with a price—feelings of tension, anxiety, and irritation most days, which can also make her vulnerable to a lowered immune system and, ultimately, illnesses.

Now let's describe another high school teacher, Ellie R. Ellie is a people pleaser. She avoids confrontations, and she is sweet and nice to everyone she meets, including her students and colleagues at her school. Always being on time is of paramount importance to her. Her reputation among the students is that not only does she give good grades, but also it's easy to talk her into raising their grades. Ellie is one of most liked teachers in her school. She has a wonderful family, and her children and husband love her dearly.

So why is Ellie so tense and unhappy? And why does she come home from school so many days feeling unhappy and unfulfilled?

TWO PERSONALITY TYPES THAT PROMOTE STRESS

The condition you are in right now largely depends upon what you have been thinking and doing to and for yourself—all your life. . . . You are the sum total of all the causes and effects you have set up in yourself through your mental and emotional attitudes.

—Bristol and Sherman (1987)

If you have several of the traits that make up either of the two personality types described in this chapter, you need not worry. The important point in the previous quote is that it is our *thinking patterns* and habits, *not* our personality traits, per se, that determine our destiny and how we react to provocations. Whether we set off our fight-or-flight response, our sympathetic nervous system (SNS), is really up to us! Because we are certainly capable of modifying and controlling our thoughts and behaviors, we don't have to become prisoners of our genetic hardwiring. But let's explore two common types of genetic hardwiring that can potentially fuel stress, if we don't recognize these traits and modify them.

Cheryl and Ellie display two very different personality types, yet both sets of traits can potentially tax their internal balance (homeostasis), even putting their physical and emotional health at risk. Again, having either one of these personalities (or for that matter, a combination of the two) is not necessarily unfortunate—what would be unfortunate is failing to modify those behaviors that are harmful, emotionally, behaviorally, or physically.

Cheryl's personality constellation fits the well-known pattern described as *Type-A personality*. The discovery and labeling of Type-A personality by two cardiologists is a fascinating story. Cardiologists Meyer Friedman and Ray

---

Good News!

Regardless of your genetically wired personality traits, you can learn to avoid switching on the SNS, which is ultimately how to control your stress.

Rosenman (1974) were running a successful practice when their office manager brought to their attention the need to reupholster the waiting-room chairs. It seems that only a few inches of the seats (toward the front edge) and the armrests of most of the chairs were worn through. The remainder of each chair was intact.

Subsequent observations of the patients in the waiting room showed that the majority of them sat on the edges of their seats, impatiently fidgeting and rubbing their hands nervously across the armrests while waiting to be called in to the examination rooms. In contrast, worn chairs were not found in the waiting rooms of other specialists, including neurologists, urologists, or oncologists; therefore, it was concluded that there must be something different about people with coronary heart disease (CHD). Accordingly, this led to a host of research studies showing the relationship between these personality traits and the onset of CHD.

One of the hallmarks of Seyle's (1976) remarkable work in the field of stress was the observation that the body needs frequent periods of quiet and calm to replenish and refresh itself. Type-A people rarely allow themselves periods of worry-free relaxation. Table 4.1 is a summary of the major traits that make up the Type-A pattern of behaviors and emotions.

Review Table 4.1, Checklist of Potential Type-A Behaviors, to see if you fit this profile.

It's important to understand that Type-A folks come with a wide variety of trait combinations, and you don't need to have all of them to fit the Type-A pattern. Check off those that apply to you.

Among all of the behaviors represented by Type-A people, the one shown in Friedman and Rosenman's (1974) original research to be most predictive of heart disease was *free-floating hostility*. Studies of a variety of occupations

Table 4.1	Checklist of Potential Type-A Behaviors

Check any that apply to you.

➤ *Sense of Time Urgency*

☐ Blinks rapidly
☐ Cuts others off in traffic
☐ Cuts others off before they finish their sentences ("uh huh . . . I know, I know")
☐ Hates lines and waiting
☐ Is impatient
☐ Multitasks to save time and to avoid forgetting anything
☐ Needs to achieve more and more in less and less time
☐ Speaks rapidly

➤ *All-or-Nothing Thinking*

☐ Thinks in black or white, perfect or failure extremes

➤ *Work Addiction*

☐ Engages in multitasking (e.g., brushes teeth while showering, scores papers while watching TV, makes notes while driving the car)
☐ Has trouble delegating
☐ Needs to be successful

> *Free-Floating Hostility*

☐ Appears insensitive to others' feelings
☐ Clenches fists during ordinary conversation
☐ Grinds teeth during sleep—facial expressions show hostility, jaw and mouth muscle tightness (jaw pain near hairline is referred to as TMJ pain)
☐ Has difficulty expressing love and feelings, except with pets
☐ Is extremely competitive—wanting to win at all costs, whether it is important or a simple game (e.g., golf)
☐ Is easily irritated
☐ Maintains an intimidating style
☐ Raises voice frequently
☐ Uses sarcasm, abrasiveness, and humor at others' expense

> *Inadequate Self-Esteem (usually unaware of this)*

☐ Displays signs of insecurity, which lies at the core of the need to prove self over and over, thus the time pressure and inability to relax
☐ Has expectations that exceed perceived achievements
☐ Micromanages for fear of failing

> *Unconscious Drive Toward Self-Destruction*

☐ Displays self-destructive behaviors, including alcohol, tobacco, and drug use to deal with anxiety
☐ Experiences vague pains and headaches often
☐ Is prone to ulcers and heart attacks

> *Need to Be in Control at All Times*

☐ Prefers to drive, rather than be a passenger to keep sense of control
☐ Makes decisions for spouse, children, *and employees* without giving them an opportunity

consistently show that having a high level of hostility predicts heart disease, hardening of the arteries, and higher death rates from these diseases, as well as higher death rates from *all* diseases.

─ Good News! ─

Regardless of the number of Type-A traits you possess, you can learn to reduce the hostility component, and once you do that, you dramatically reduce the risk for heart disease.

Simplify your life. Ask yourself what really needs to be done. If you don't perform a specific task right now, what's the worst that will happen? Get a good Spam blocker so you can avoid having to read the bulk of your e-mails, and be selective regarding the number of people to whom you give your e-mail address. Read Lakein's How to Get Control of Your Time and Your Life *(1973).*

Learn to be flexible and just go with the flow. As the Quaker proverb goes, "In the face of strong winds, let me be a blade of grass. In the face of strong walls, let me be a gale of wind" (Sapolsky, 1998, p. 416).

Ellie's personality constellation is very different, but it's just as stressful and harmful to her emotional and physical health. Ellie's personality structure fits closely with what has been termed the *people-pleasing personality*, and she pays a big price for maintaining some of her traits. A person with this pattern of traits exhibits the behavioral tendencies listed in Table 4.2.

Table 4.2   Checklist of Potential People-Pleasing Behaviors

Check any that apply to you.

➤ *Desires and Needs Everyone's Approval*
 	
   ☐ Is vulnerable to being manipulated and taken advantage of because of the strong desire to be liked
   ☐ Rarely pleased or satisfied with self
   ☐ Will risk an accident rather than be late for an event because, "What will they think of me if I'm late?"
 	
➤ *Avoids Confrontations—Not Assertive*
 	
   ☐ Agrees with others and goes with the flow, rather than challenge anyone
   ☐ Has difficulty returning items to stores
   ☐ Has difficulty sending food back in restaurants
   ☐ Rationalizes nonassertive reactions to incidents (e.g., "It wasn't the waiter's fault that the food wasn't cooked correctly, so I didn't want to upset him by asking him to cook my food longer.")
 	
➤ *Avoids Expressing Criticism—Not Assertive*
 	
   ☐ Feels guilty turning people down for favors
   ☐ Is hesitant to say no to people
   ☐ Is hesitant to show anger and disappointment, even when it is justified (sometimes avoids showing anger because of fear of exploding)

☐ Wants to be seen by others as nice *and believes that disagreeing or expressing self assertively equates to not being nice*

➤ *Suffers From Self-Doubt, Insecurity, and Fear*

☐ Afraid of making decisions (to avoid mistakes) and seeks the advice of others, rather than trusting own judgment

☐ Avoids conflict at all costs, thus playing a charade in relationships

☐ Believes that pleasing others and being seen as nice will avoid negative feedback

☐ Doesn't risk being real and expressing negative emotions

☐ Fears rejection, abandonment, conflict, and loneliness

☐ Has problems in relationships because of rarely giving feedback to others about what *behavior is offensive or hurtful*

☐ Misjudges others' behavior as being "mad at me"

☐ Second-guesses self constantly

☐ Self-doubt and fear remain because the person doesn't risk being "real" with others

➤ *Stuffs Negative Emotions Down, Ignoring Them*

☐ Vulnerable to *implosions*—the body pays the price of not expressing negative emotions

☐ Examples of physiological consequences of repressed emotions are migraines, gastrointestinal problems, back pain, chronic-fatigue syndrome, and alcohol and substance abuse

People pleasers are often vulnerable to being taken advantage of and manipulated. Moreover, they are hurting themselves by avoiding negative emotions at all costs. The most common chronic problems for people pleasers are sadness and internal physical upheaval.

Dunham and Varma (1998) point to many research findings connecting specific personality traits of teachers to physiological stress outcomes. Socially anxious, introverted teachers have exaggerated stress responses to the task of teaching, with neck muscle tension predominating. More socially comfortable extroverts, on the other hand, seem to have effective coping responses to the same tasks and suffer less stress.

Timid, noncompetitive teachers who habitually think about fear-producing situations related to their jobs are the most prone to feeling inadequate and lack coping skills.

┌ Good News! ─────────────────

You are a prisoner of *neither* your genetics nor your upbringing. Once you recognize your stress provocations and your self-defeating, emotionally inappropriate thinking patterns, you can begin to change in a very healthy way, regardless of the personality traits you have exhibited all of your life.

If you have Type-A or people-pleasing personality characteristics or any of the other traits described earlier, fear not. Next, you will find methods of modifying *any* behaviors that are making you more prone to stress.

YOU CAN START MODIFYING SOME OF YOUR TYPE-A BEHAVIORS TODAY!

Type-A behavior—however induced and however deep-seated— can be changed by the individual himself or herself, and we have proved it.

—Meyer Friedman and Nancy Ulmer *(1984)*

Rx 16
Stress Mastery

The next time you feel any negative emotion, revisit Table 4.1 to see if you are engaging in these behaviors.

Allow me to reiterate that if you are a Type-A person you don't need to change your whole personality, which you couldn't do even if you wished to. However, there is much research, cited by Friedman and Rosenman (1974) and Roskies (1987) that shows that Type-A folks typically respond to stress in ways that lead to CHD. When discussing the reasons for increased CHD in Type-A people, Roskies (1987) notes the following:

> *In response to certain types of challenge and threat, Type-A people tend to show greater elevations in blood pressure, heart rate, cortisol, epinephrine, and norepinephrine than Type Bs. . . . Episodic elevations in blood pressure and heart rate are thought to damage the inner layer of the coronary arteries, thereby contributing to atherosclerosis and subsequent CHD. (p. 20)*

Type-A folks possess many wonderful characteristics, including creativity, drive, persistence, and attention to detail. In fact, Friedman and Ulmer (1984) cite a study in which they determined that large percentages of Type-A people were found in a variety of respected professions, including the following:

- University presidents,
- Bank presidents,

- Corporation chairpersons,
- Generals and admirals,
- Archbishops, bishops, and rabbis,
- Nobel laureates,
- Congressmen and senators, and
- Federal judges.

Actually, we find successful Type-A people in virtually all of the professions, including teaching, medicine, law, and engineering. However, Friedman and Ulmer (1984) are quick to point out large percentages of people they labeled *Type-B*, who also are successful in these professions. In other words, you don't need to hold onto harmful Type-A traits in order to maintain your success! If you are a Type-A person, it's not your time urgency, impatience, hostility, or need to be in control that makes you a success. In fact, those traits are usually counterproductive to success. Friedman and Ulmer suggest that your success is more likely because of your creativity, decision-making, confidence, organizational skills, and drive to accomplish your goals.

Type-B people, in general, do not have a sense of time urgency, give themselves time to contemplate, relax, and "recharge their batteries," feel good about themselves and maintain good self-esteem, don't get irritated with the inadequacies of their subordinates, don't demonstrate free-floating hostility, and they are usually able to cope with stress quite effectively.

A common objection raised by Type-A people when it is suggested that they consider changing some of their behaviors is "I was born this way, my father (or mother) is this way, and I can't become a different person." The intent is never to change your personality. Many of our behavioral habits feel like they are part of our personalities because we have always acted that way, but our self-talk and behavioral habits are *learned* over time. This is very important to know because anything that is learned can be unlearned. Modifying habits or learning new ones does not mean a complete makeover. You don't need to throw out the baby with the bathwater. You can choose to *modify* those behaviors and habits that are working against you, without having to become a completely different person.

Another objection often raised by Type-A people is that "I don't want to mess with success. I'm happy being a Type-A person. It's worked for me up until now, so why should I change?" The answer to this objection is that once you modify those behaviors and habits that are potentially harmful, you will continue to work with the same enthusiasm, creativity, and zeal, but without the stress, which so often accompanies your work.

So let's talk about modifying behaviors and habits. In Chapter 3, I discussed how we tend to *awfulize* to ourselves when we face situations that we interpret negatively, resulting in painful emotions. These unfortunate ways of thinking persist because we are creatures of habit. But, as you now understand, our thinking patterns can certainly be challenged and changed.

In Chapter 1, I referenced research that shows that 75% to 90% of all illnesses and physical symptoms are stress related (AIS, n.d.), and Dr. Helmstetter (1982) describes research stating that up to 75% of our thoughts are negative and counterproductive, ultimately contributing to the onset or exacerbation of many of these unwanted physical and emotional outcomes. As you now know, once you recognize your negative thinking patterns, you *can* change them.

It follows, then, that once you recognize and understand your Type-A behaviors, and understand that modifying these behaviors and feelings and attitudes is *under your control,* you can actually make changes that will make a *real difference* in your life and health. Here are some practical prescriptions for behaviors that you can build into your daily routine to modify Type-A components.

Become aware of the triggers to your stress feelings.

You can easily identify the daily hassles in and out of school that trigger stress feelings. Is it a particular student, the principal sitting in class, being assigned extra duties, traffic frustrations, or something else? Using the checklist in Table 4.3, you can list all of the specific triggers you are aware of and rate the level of tension you feel with each—either mild, moderate, or high.

Find a relaxation technique you're comfortable with, and make it part of your daily routine. See Resource C for a relaxation example. Practice your relaxation skills in a place where you will be left alone and not interrupted by the phone, TV, or other people.

Besides the method described in the Resource C, you can use any relaxation routine you are comfortable with, including yoga, meditation, and even self-hypnosis. If you use the technique in Resource C, you simply read the words slowly into a recorder, and then play the recording back for yourself frequently. The recording will only be 12 to 15 minutes long, so it won't take much of your time, but it will be a powerful tool for you, if you make a habit of listening to it. The best time to practice relaxation is either before you go to school or as soon as you get home. Try to develop the habit of practicing daily, perhaps rotating different techniques so you don't get bored with a single method.

Table 4.3	Checklist of Potential Stress Triggers and the Level of Tension Generated by Each

Check all that apply to you, and add other triggers you are aware of. Check the tension level: mild, moderate, or high, for each trigger.

Stress Triggers	Level of Tension		
School-Related + Out of School	*Mild*	*Moderate*	*High*
☐ A particular student's personality and/or behavior			
☐ My principal asking to meet with me			
☐ Being forced to take on extra duties			
☐ Deadlines for completing paperwork			
☐ Being told that a parent is waiting for a return call from me			
☐ Anticipating a stressful parent-teacher conference			
☐ Dealing with a hostile coworker			
☐ Traffic to and from school			
☐ Dealing with my spouse's needs			
☐ Dealing with my children's needs			
☐ Long lines at the supermarket or bank			
☐ Cooking for my family			
☐			
☐			
☐			

Use short relaxation exercises several times a day.

Besides the 12- to 15-minute relaxation technique you employ each day, you can use an abbreviated version (1–2 minutes) several times a day. Pick out what works fastest for you from the longer session found in Resource C. For example, if you enjoy the muscle tensing and releasing routine, you can use an abbreviated muscle tensing and releasing program to prepare yourself for a potentially tension-producing situation, such as the principal coming into your class in an hour.

A minute of deep breathing and muscle tensing and releasing can go a long way toward relaxing you in advance. If you enjoy imagining a relaxing scene, take some deep, relaxing breaths and go to the scene for a minute or two.

You can also use either of these shortened versions as a first step in regaining self-control whenever you find yourself in a state of high tension.

Get in touch with your false beliefs and change them.

These are beliefs that may underlie your issues with impatience and time urgency. For example, you may believe that "My diligence directed at always being on time has helped me become successful in my teaching career." It's almost as if someone told you that it's your impatience and irritation that has made you such a wonderful teacher! This false belief comes from not understanding the real reasons you are successful, such as your intelligence, creativity, ability to make a curriculum interesting, persistence, and motivation—not because you are impatient and get all of your work done precisely on time! You would undoubtedly be even *more successful* if you recharged your batteries with relaxing breaks several times each day.

Getting in touch with false beliefs also means understanding the irrational self-talk that is involved in each situation and challenging (rebutting) that talk. Table 4.4 provides examples and spaces for you to enter stress-provoking situations that occur in your life.

Second, rate the tension level **(C)** you feel in the next column. This is the combination of the provocation and the resultant critical self-talk **(B)**, which sets off (triggers) that tension. The critical final step is providing yourself with rational, disputing (rebuttal) self-talk **(D)**. Write down as many rebuttal thoughts as you can think of in the box on the far right.

Once you see that your rebuttal thoughts make much more sense and are much more logical than your original thoughts, your tension level should reduce dramatically. This is the ultimate result of rationally rethinking your situation. By writing down these provoking situations whenever you are aware of them, noting your self-talk and especially your *rebuttal* self-talk, you will ultimately develop the habit of engaging in positive, rational thinking whenever you have a provocative situation, resulting in keeping your stress and tension levels manageable.

Table 4.4 Stress Provocations, Critical Self-Talk Triggers, and Disputed Self-Talk

Make copies of this table before you fill it in so that you will have tables to fill in every time you feel stressed.

Provocative Situation (A)	Tension Level (C)	Critical Self-Talk (Trigger) (B)	Disputed Self-Talk (Rebuttal) (D)
1. My most challenging student had a melt-down in class and was completely out of control.	High	1. "I hate this kid. He is making my life miserable. I feel completely helpless and can't control him. He will always disrupt my class. I can't handle this stress."	1. "I don't have to be perfect and be able to control every single child in my class. I will bring this case up in a staff meeting and get others' input about working with this child."
2. My principal has asked to meet with me after school.	High	2. "What now? I'm tired of his criticism, and I believe he's going to punish me with more extra duties."	2. "I don't know for sure that he is calling me in to criticize me. I'll just see what happens, and if there is criticism, I will assert myself, like I have been practicing."
3. I can't stand the traffic to and from school.	Moderate	3. "I have to leave my home so early to get to school on time, and I'm so exhausted by the time I get home."	3. "I know I have no control over the traffic. I can practice my relaxation skills while driving and can bring calming and comforting CDs to play while the traffic is stalled. I can also prepare snacks to bring with me on the way home, to energize me after the long school day."
4. My spouse and children demand too much of my time.	Moderate	4. "They just don't understand how drained I am when I get home, and then I have to grade papers and prepare for the next day. I just can't be pulled in any more directions!"	4. "My spouse and children love me, and I'm a very important part of their lives. I will budget my time to allow for some special time for each of them, without feeling guilty about spending that time away from my schoolwork."
5.			
6.			

Adapted from Matthew McKay and Martha Davis. *Thoughts and Feelings.*, 1981, with permission from Harbinger Press.

67

Recognize the price you are paying to achieve more and more in less and less time.

When the underlying goal is to achieve more and more, the downside is that you are preoccupied with your own activities and ignoring the needs of the people around you. Think about the time your spouse, children, and friends are missing because of this unfortunate habit. So start taking an interest in the lives of those around you. *Take the time to listen to them,* and show them that they are important to you. (See also Stress Mastery Prescription 29)

Get a time-management book, and practice the techniques you learn from it.

An even better idea is to take a time-management course. Get rid of the relatively unimportant minutiae that fill your weekly schedule and prioritize relaxation, family time, and reading into your weekly schedule. Examine your routines, and objectively determine which ones you can let go of without disastrous effects. This also addresses the important issue of balancing your career and your life. Recognize how balancing your career with your family or off-the-job interests will help you succeed in the long run because the off-the-job activities will make you whole. Go ahead and *take a risk* by spending relaxing time with family, friends, and yourself each week, without allowing work to interfere and without feeling guilty in the process! You'll soon realize how much *more productive* you will be in your career.

Here are additional tips:

Never skip or shorten breakfast.

Nutritionists point out the critical value of eating a good breakfast. Don't make this the hurried beginning to a hurried day. Enjoy it with family members, and model the appropriate breakfast behavior for your children. Make sure it's a nutritious breakfast, such as including a protein shake, which doesn't take long to prepare.

Take multiple minibreaks during the day.

Break up your work routine by taking the time to go for a walk, meditate, or listen to soothing music or your relaxation routine on your iPod or portable CD player.

What you gain by recharging your batteries in this way will be far more beneficial for you than the time the 10 minutes, or so, each break takes.

Make a deal with yourself that you will never leave school later than 5:00 p.m. (unless you have an additional duty).

Clean off your desk when you leave so you will come in to an uncluttered desk the next morning. Taking the pressure off yourself to keep working is literally reducing the chances of the onset of diseases, which will ultimately cost you much more time.

Try hard to eliminate multitasking.

Do one activity at a time, rather than cramming everything in at once. *Listen* to what colleagues, students, and parents are saying to you without simultaneously thinking about other things that you need to get done. Get used to focusing your complete attention on one task at a time. If you're worried that you'll forget to do something, get a pad of paper at the nearest printing store that says, "Things to Do Today" across the top of each sheet. Have a box next to each line you write on so you can have fun checking off each item once you complete it. This will ensure that you won't forget anything so you can do one thing at a time without fear of forgetting.

Pay attention to your angry and hostile behaviors, and learn to modify them using anger-mastery techniques.

Now you know that the free-floating hostility component of many Type-A people's personalities is the most dangerous risk factor for CHD. Although anger management is beyond the scope of this book, there are many excellent books that cover anger management, including, my favorite, McKay and Rogers (1985). In addition, I have a hypnotic anger-mastery series that was just produced (Singer, 2009).

Here is a tip to get you started: *Get an objective handle on when and how you react with anger and hostility.* Ask your spouse, teaching colleagues, and friends to be honest with you and tell you when you act angry or hostile. Ask them to be as specific as possible so you will understand exactly how they see you, even though you may not see these behaviors in yourself. Just as with stress, it's crucial to understand the self-talk triggers that set off your anger.

As you can see in Table 4.5, you can examine each situation in which you feel anger and frustration **(A)**, determine the self-talk that triggered you **(B)**, and dispute (rebuttal) that self-talk **(D)** to reduce your hostile emotional and behavioral responses to the situation (C1 and C2), which are not included in this table. The ultimate outcomes **(E)** when you engage in such disputed self-talk (rebuttals) are healthy stress-reducing consequences.

Table 4.5	Anger Provocations, Critical Self-Talk Triggers, Disputed Self-Talk, and Ultimate Outcomes

Make copies of this table before you fill it in, so you will have tables to fill in every time you feel angry.

Provocative Situation (A)	Critical Self-Talk (Trigger) (B)	Disputed Self-Talk (Rebuttal) (D)	Ultimate Outcomes (E)
1. My principal comes into my class unannounced to observe me.	1. "This is not fair. I didn't know she was coming in, and I'm not as prepared as I should be. This really angers me!"	1. "She is just doing her job. She isn't trying to catch me screwing up; she really hopes I do well. My job is to always come to class prepared and do what I do best—teach and have fun doing it."	1. Once I started to talk to myself rationally, and reviewing my lesson plan each evening, I actually hoped she'd come and observe me. There is really nothing here that I need to be angry about.
2. I have a class clown who defies me and loves disrupting my class.	2. "This student has absolutely no respect for me and enjoys embarrassing me and disrupting the class. He manages to get me to yell at him almost every day. I hate this child."	2. "I need to talk privately with this student and find out why he needs all of this attention. Perhaps I can put him on a progress report system where I will e-mail his parents each day about his ability to control himself, and they can have a consequence chart for him. This child doesn't have it in for me; he just wants all of the	2. I was able to get his parents in for a conference, and we planned a behavioral intervention using my progress report e-mail system. I felt wonderful that I was able to creatively solve this problem, and I am much calmer every day in class now.

Provocative Situation (A)	Critical Self-Talk (Trigger) (B)	Disputed Self-Talk (Rebuttal) (D)	Ultimate Outcomes (E)
		attention he can get. Maybe this progress report system will give him healthy attention, and he'll stop disrupting the class."	
3. Some of my colleagues criticize my teaching style during staff meetings.	3. "They have some nerve criticizing me. I could say plenty about the way they teach, but I mind my own business. This really angers me about them."	3. "I know that I'm a good teacher, and I really care about the privilege of impacting the lives of my students. Knowing that I'll never be able to please everyone all of the time, I choose to disregard criticism from those colleagues who want to embarrass me in front of everyone in the staff meeting."	3. Disregarding the complaints coming from a few negative colleagues and focusing on the positive feedback coming from the others has really taken the pressure off of me, and I'm no longer hostile, even to my negative colleagues. I politely say 'thanks' and go about my business.
4.			
5.			

Adapted from Matthew McKay and Martha Davis. *Thoughts and Feelings.*, 1981, with permission from Harbinger Press.

Again, it's very important to recognize the statements you are saying to yourself when you are feeling angry or frustrated. Then, give yourself more calming, peaceful, rational rebuttals, and your anger should be reduced dramatically. So, practice writing down situations that provoke your anger and frustration each day in Table 4.5, under Provocative Situation **(A)**. Then record your self-talk triggers and disputed self-talk. This will eventually lead to positive, rational thinking that should really help prevent or remediate your angry emotions.

Even though it may be embarrassing, it will help to share this list of anger-provoking situations with your spouse or good friend because that person will be able to give you an objective view of the situation. Hopefully, this will help you see when you tend to overreact.

You now know about *free-floating hostility*. This is continual anger and irritability without a specific cause or provocation, expressed frequently, even in trivial situations, and often in subtle ways, such as through sarcasm or humor at others' expense. Tips for eliminating this free-floating hostility are contained in Table 4.6.

Table 4.6   Ten Tips for Eliminating Free-Floating Hostility

Check all that apply to you.

☐ *Tell your spouse, colleagues, and friends that you realize you are carrying around free-floating hostility and that you plan to eliminate it. (This will help you commit to it, just like announcing a weight-loss goal to these people. Have a prearranged signal for them to give you when they notice you are getting hot under the collar.)*

☐ *Regularly express appreciation to these people for helping you to recognize and manage these emotions.*

☐ *Regularly express love and affection to your spouse and children, and freely express to your friends and colleagues how much you value them.*

☐ *Surprise one of these people at least once a month with tickets to a movie, concert, or the like. Your spouse was once your sweetheart. Start treating her or him like that again.*

☐ *Examine the opinions of people with whom you disagree, from their perspective, before judging them.*

☐ *When playing games for fun with your spouse and children, stop being so competitive, and try to allow them to experience the joy of winning.*

☐ *Look in a mirror several times a day to see if your face exhibits anger, frustration, or irritation. Practice smiling in the mirror, and memorize the muscles in your laughing face so you can display it during the day. (See if your forehead is wrinkled and your eyebrows turned down and look for muscle tension. Then get into the habit of smiling more.)*

> ☐ *Go to sporting events, where it's socially acceptable to yell and scream your guts out! (Get it out of your system.)*
>
> ☐ *Each evening ask yourself what you did to show kindness to someone.*
>
> ☐ *Deliberately admit that you're wrong in as many situations as you can, and write the situations down.*

Practice active-listening techniques.

How to Use Active-Listening Skills

One of the problems that many Type-A people have is that they do not really listen to people with whom they are communicating. Their minds are filled with other agendas, and they have a tendency to want to control the dialogue, rather than have an open exchange. *Active listening* means being patient and paying close attention to the messages that people are communicating to you. Because Type-A people are so often impatient, they frequently finish others' sentences for them, as if they are saying to themselves, "I get it, so you don't have to finish." This leads to projecting their own ideas onto the communicator and into the message, thus, incorrectly assuming its intent.

Here is a model for practicing active-listening skills:

Ask gentle questions to understand what the speaker is trying to say and the emotions involved. For example, you could ask, "Are you angry because you don't think I took your ideas into consideration before making my decision?"

Reflect back or paraphrase what you heard before responding or commenting on it. If you were not listening to the meaning, the other people will clarify your paraphrase. It's important not to respond until they agree that your interpretation of what they were saying is correct.

When you are listening, don't be doing other things, such as shuffling papers. Always maintain eye contact with the speaker and sit on the same level, rather than one of you standing while the other sits.

Watch for nonverbal behavior (body language, facial expressions). Scientific research shows that body language, expressions, and tone of voice will often give you more information about the message than their words. In terms of your own body language, when you are listening, lean forward toward the speaker, breathing easily, and remain relaxed. Tenseness and frowning on your part suggests that you are angry, frustrated, or impatient with the speaker.

Acknowledge the message you are hearing; you don't have to agree—just acknowledge what you hear the speaker saying. Put yourself in the shoes of other speakers, and try to see where they are coming from, even if you don't agree. Just listen and understand. A nod here and there also communicates that you are listening; however, it may also indicate to the speaker that you agree with what is being said, so be selective with your nods.

Don't feel pressed to have an answer. Tell speakers you'll think about what they are asking and get back with them the next day, for example. Avoid your tendency to be impatient and rush an answer that you may later regret.

Always allow the speaker to finish. You may need to take notes if the speaker is long-winded, but be patient, rather than interrupt, roll your eyes, or get frustrated.

YOU CAN START MODIFYING SOME OF YOUR PEOPLE-PLEASING BEHAVIORS TODAY!

You can stop the progression of the disease to please, and you can change now.

—Harriet Braiker (1995)

Review the people-pleasing behaviors in Table 4.2 to see if you fit this profile.

Table 4.7 lists the specific beliefs that underlie people-pleasing behaviors. As you can imagine, maintaining such beliefs makes it difficult to *risk* changing behaviors. For example, believing that "I must avoid confrontations at all costs" will prevent you from standing up for yourself in many situations.

You can see that these beliefs are self-defeating. You need to understand that the reason people like you is *not* because you always say *yes*. You are a good person, and they like you because of your values, not because you always accommodate them.

Learn how to assert yourself without feeling guilty.

Table 4.7	Checklist of 10 Common People-Pleasing Beliefs

Check all that apply to you.

- ❏ I need to be adored by everyone.
- ❏ I need to avoid confrontations at all costs.
- ❏ I should never have negative feelings or emotions regarding anyone in my life.
- ❏ I believe that others should treat me the way I treat them.
- ❏ I believe that if I don't disappoint people, they shouldn't criticize or reject me.
- ❏ I believe that because I am so nice to others, they should never hurt me, be angry with me, or treat me unfairly.
- ❏ I should strive to always do what others want, expect, or need from me, even if it hurts me in the process.
- ❏ Putting other's feelings ahead of mine makes me a good person.
- ❏ I should never say no to people or disappoint them.
- ❏ There is a reward waiting for me in heaven for being such a nice person to everyone and putting them first, ahead of me.

How to Assert Yourself

Most of the time, we communicate with others in one of three ways: aggressively, nonassertively, or assertively. For the Type-A person, aggressive communication is common; for the people pleaser, nonassertive communication is the predominant method.

Nonassertive responses involve not sharing your true feelings and trying to

> **Good News!**
>
> There are many assertiveness skills that you can begin practicing *right now*, and asserting yourself will make a huge difference in the way you feel about yourself.

accommodate others' requests or agree with their point of view, regardless of how you *really* feel. These responses reflect weakness and the belief that you don't have the right, power, or ability to stand up for yourself.

Nonassertive people are often apologetic when they ask for something and frequently sprinkle their language with self-deprecating comments, such as, "This is probably a stupid idea, but . . ." They also avoid beginning a sentence with the word "I" and prefer to deflect attention from their feelings and emotions.

On the other hand, *aggressive* responses involve trying to overpower the other person, proving you are right, regardless of whether you are insulting or embarrassing the other person.

Assertive responses are based on an attitude that *you* are just as entitled to express your true feelings as anyone with whom you are communicating. Assertiveness means being open and direct about how you feel, without feeling anxiety or guilt. Many nonassertive people feel uncomfortable even giving compliments and positive feedback to others, so assertiveness involves being able to express *all* emotions without discomfort.

But being assertive also means that you have the freedom to choose whether assertive behavior is appropriate in a particular situation. There may be times when it is not in your best interest to assert yourself. For example, if your principal arrived at school very upset about what happened at home, that may not be the appropriate time to assert yourself in criticizing a decision the principal made the day before. Common sense dictates using all of the information at hand when deciding when and where to assert yourself. The key is to know that you made a rational decision to delay your request, rather than delaying it simply because you were uncomfortable asserting yourself.

Maintaining the people-pleasing behavior of nonassertiveness can take as big a toll on your emotional and physical well-being, as do many Type-A traits. Table 4.8 points out the dangers of maintaining these beliefs.

Table 4.8   Dangers Inherent in People-Pleasing Beliefs

- Review Chapter 3. You will quickly recognize that all of these beliefs are examples of illogical, distorted thinking, including should statements, mind reading, fortune-telling, emotional reasoning, labeling, and overgeneralizing. With distorted thinking, you set yourself up for disappointment, confusion, and self-blame when you don't get the results you desire.
- Because these beliefs and denials of reality force you to swallow negative emotions, thoughts, and behaviors (or at least not show them to others), you cause implosions inside your body, leading to illnesses, a compromised immune system, and emotional distress.
- Because you avoid confrontations at all costs, you are encouraging those around you to repeat the same behaviors that hurt you. If you don't give

How to Thrive Despite Being Genetically Wired With Stress-Prone Personality Traits   77

them the feedback about how you feel, they will never know. They cannot read your mind.

- Because you hold onto a rigid set of beliefs about how people should behave toward you, you invite a life of frustration, disappointment, anger, and resentment.
- Because most of the people with whom you come in contact are not like you, you feel confused, frustrated, and discouraged by their behavior. You constantly have to live a double standard, where you treat others with total reverence and respect and somehow rationalize why they don't treat you the same way.
- Because you rationalize that these nonassertive traits are appropriate to teach your children, you are devastated when they say no to you or show angry emotions. You may be quick to blame yourself or your spouse as parental failures because your children are not people pleasers like you.

Note: For more information about these dangers, see Braiker, 1995.

To help you recognize your assertiveness choices, use the form in Table 4.9 and describe each situation where you had a choice but behaved nonassertively.

If you find yourself lacking in assertiveness, there are many steps you can take, starting right now, to modify these behaviors and habits. In Table 4.9, use the **A-B-C** model once again. Describe the situation in as much detail as possible **(A)**, including what you were feeling emotionally, what you were saying to yourself about the situation **(B)**, and what the consequences of your nonassertive behaviors were **(C)**. Next, be sure to record the eventual outcome of your behaving nonassertively **(E)**.

As you become attuned to situations in your life that call for assertive responses, where you reacted in a nonassertive manner, you will become sensitive to those situations in the future.

So what else can you do to modify your behaviors to become more assertive? Read a good self-help guide, such as those by Braiker (1995) or Fensterheim and Baer (1975). Braiker's book includes a 21-day action plan for overcoming people-pleasing habits. In their classic book, Fensterheim and Baer give a whole host of ideas for standing up for your right to take care of yourself (asserting yourself) and not feeling as if you must succumb to every request that is made of you. Many times, people pleasers are all-or-nothing thinkers, and they would prefer succumbing to saying no, which they actually view as an aggressive response.

Table 4.9   My Nonassertive Response Record

Make copies of this table before you fill it in so you will have tables to fill in every time you behave in a nonassertive fashion. In the first row, you will find a sample of how to use this table.

The Date, the Situation, and My Emotions (A)	My Self-Talk (B)	How I Handled the Situation (C)	The Eventual Outcome (E)
Friday 1. I have had plans to go to the lake this weekend with a good friend. My assistant principal approached me at school today and said she could really use my help setting up her garage sale over the weekend. I felt tense all over when she asked for my help.	1. "I'll be letting her down if I tell her I can't help her this weekend." "She may change her feelings about me." "I hope my friend doesn't get angry with me for changing our plans."	1. I called my friend and explained that I just couldn't turn down my assistant principal, and we could go to the lake the next weekend.	1. My friend said that once I commit to a plan, I should stick to it. She said she couldn't go next weekend. I felt really awful, but what else could I do?
2.			
3.			

On the contrary, saying no is actually an assertive response, not an aggressive one. An aggressive decline is filled with harshness, sarcasm, and vitriol and often offends the other person. So when your gut tells you that you really don't want to do what someone is requesting of you, do the following:

Delay giving an answer. Give yourself at least a day to think about the situation, rather than quickly responding yes and then feeling the pressure to do something you really don't want to do. Say you need some time to consider this. This time gives you a feeling of being in control and a chance to rehearse your response. For example, you could say, "I understand your concerns and what you are asking, but I would like some time to think about it and gather more information before I give you an answer."

Separate people who are asking from the task they are requesting. Realize that by saying no you are rejecting *the task,* not the person making the request of you. So if your principal is asking if you'll volunteer for an additional after-school duty, you can say, "I really appreciate your trusting me for that duty, but I can't take on any more tasks right now." You don't need to explain any further, and you *do not* need to apologize for refusing the request.

Decide whether the request or invitation is really in your best interest. What is your true feeling about this request? Being honest with yourself, do you really want to do this?

Think about the most likely consequences of saying yes. This is an important decision point. Would saying yes to this request cause any problem for you? If it would, you should politely decline, given the expected consequences of doing so. After deliberating the consequences, if you decide to say yes to the request, realize that you made an assertive decision because you stopped and considered all of the likely consequences first.

Express your thoughts, opinions, beliefs, and interpretations. State your thoughts and feelings with "I" statements. These statements are assertive expressions of your feelings and decisions, whereas "you" statements are confrontational and accusatory. For example, if your colleague or partner is constantly leaving late for a meeting or engagement, say, "I really get upset when I'm late, and it's important for me to be on time," instead of, "You're always making me late."

State what you want without using words like "always" and "never." These words are exaggerations and often make people react to you defensively.

Often you understand the requester's position and need while also wanting to take care of your needs, so try to find a workable compromise. Compromises can involve doing it their way this time and yours the next, or you'll do this if they'll do something for you in return, or you'll do part of what they want and part of what you want.

Continue to use your favorite relaxation technique. When you are asserting yourself, it's quite helpful to remain relaxed and in control of your emotions, so keep practicing relaxation techniques.

Take notice of and keep a record of situations in which you were assertive and reward yourself accordingly.

Now let's focus on those times in which you were in a situation that invited an assertive response and you actually chose to do so. Use Table 4.10 to record these instances, your self-talk, how you handled the situations, and the eventual outcomes.

Here are some examples of low-anxiety producing ways to begin asserting yourself:

Go into a fast-food establishment (e.g., Burger King) and order only a cup of water. Do not order any food. Trust me, they will gladly had you a cup and direct you to the water, without any hard feelings.

Go into a store and ask for change for a dollar. Do *not* purchase anything. Again, this is your perfect right, and there is no need for you to feel guilty or think you are being unfair to the clerk.

Ask a stranger for the time. The best place to do this is in a store or mall. Don't ask, "Do you have the time?" It's better to assert yourself with, "I would appreciate it if you would tell me the time . . . thanks."

Force yourself to engage in small talk with someone you don't know very well. Perhaps after a staff meeting or at a social gathering you can practice this by approaching someone you'd like to know better and introducing yourself.

When people compliment you or your clothing, politely say, "Thank you." Don't defuse the compliment with a negative or disparaging remark about yourself or your clothing.

Compliment people at work. Giving compliments is a great way to begin asserting yourself. This is really a no-lose scenario because everyone loves to receive genuine compliments, and they will like you for doing so.

Look people in the eye when you speak to them. If that is difficult for you, imagine a cross on their forehead and look at the cross. People will perceive that you're looking right into their eyes, and as you get more comfortable with this, you can eventually lower your focus right into their eyes.

Reward yourself with really positive self-talk. After accomplishing each assertive act, talk to yourself with really positive and complimentary comments, such as, "I'm really proud of myself and this feels really good."

Table 4.10   My Assertive-Response Record

Make copies of this table before you fill it in, so you will have tables to fill in every time you behave in an assertive fashion. In the first row, you will find a sample of how to use this table.

The Date, the Situation, and My Emotions (A)	My Self-Talk (B)	How I Handled the Situation (C)	The Eventual Outcomes (E)
Sunday 1. Mother calls and tells me that her friend's daughters come to visit them much more frequently than I do. I feel really angry and guilty at the same time.	1. "My mother is disappointed in me. Maybe she's right, and I'm a lousy daughter."	1. I told my mother that I understand that she is lonely. I love her very much and will spend as much time with her as I can. I would like her to respect me and my needs and not judge me harshly when I don't spend as much time with her as she would like me to.	1. My mother seemed surprised to hear me say that. It actually felt good to stand up for myself. She was upset at first, but then seemed to be calm and asked when I thought I could see her. I felt wonderful being able to share my emotions with her without fear.
2.			
3.			
4.			

Treat yourself to something special once you have accumulated five assertive acts, such as buying something you really want but have disciplined yourself to waiting for until you "earned" it.

Let's get back to Cheryl M. and Ellie R., the two teachers with Type-A and people-pleasing personalities, respectively. Although Cheryl's students did consistently well because of her compulsive practice of drilling them incessantly, she began to receive negative feedback from parents about her temper and sarcasm in the classroom. Cheryl took the advice of a friend and took an evening anger-management course at a local community college. This was an eye-opening experience for her, and she actually used her needs to be in control and to be perfect to thrive in this course.

The course lasted three months, and at the conclusion of it, her colleagues, who didn't realize she was taking the course, were amazed at the transformation she made, in and out of the classroom. Yes, she *was* ultimately named Teacher of the Year.

Ellie's people-pleasing behaviors began to take a toll on her body. She missed many days at school because of vague symptoms, which her doctors couldn't diagnose, let alone cure. Of course, this worried her even more, and her stress level continued to rise. Eventually, Ellie confided in her best friend (another teacher) about how unhappy she was. Ellie admitted that she frequently allowed herself to be manipulated into doing things she was uncomfortable with, by her principal, students' parents, and even by some of her students. Her friend was stunned because Ellie always had a smile on her face and a warm demeanor with her students, colleagues, and parents.

This friend convinced Ellie to get professional help. Ultimately, Ellie's psychologist diagnosed her disease-to-please personality pattern and showed her how keeping her feelings in and presenting a facade was causing internal disruption in her body. He suggested that Ellie check the continuing education offerings at a local junior college for a course in personal growth and development. Bam! Ellie discovered a course in assertiveness training. The rest is history.

Ellie began saying no when she didn't want to do something and stood her ground with folks who had learned to expect her to comply with their wishes. Ellie even began to become more assertive with her husband and her teenage children. Her stress level in general and at school, in particular, reduced dramatically, and she enjoyed her job like never before.

Once Ellie learned to assert herself and take charge of her feelings in interacting with others, her physical symptoms dramatically improved. And guess what? She was still adored (and now highly respected) by her students and colleagues!

ACTION PLAN FOR STRESS MASTERY

| Table 4.11 | Action Plan for Stress Mastery |

Check each that you accomplish.	
New Behavior	*What I Did and the Date Accomplished*
❏ I will use the Type-A behavior checklist to determine whether I exhibit any of these behaviors and if so, I will use the steps discussed in this chapter to modify those behaviors that are detrimental to my stress level. ❏ ❏ ❏	What I did: Date accomplished:
❏ I will use the people-pleasing checklist to determine whether I have exhibited any of these behaviors and if so, I will use the steps discussed in this chapter to modify those behaviors that are detrimental to my stress level. ❏ ❏ ❏	What I did: Date accomplished:
❏ I will explore the stress triggers in my life (both in and out of school), and I will determine the level of tension caused by each. ❏ ❏ ❏	What I did: Date accomplished:
❏ I will use my tables to examine the triggers to my stress and anger and practice disputing the self-talk that leads to my stress and anger. ❏ ❏ ❏	What I did: Date accomplished:

(Continued)

Table 4.11	(Continued)	
❐ I will use my tables to record my nonassertive responses and practice using assertive responses. ❐ ❐ ❐	What I did: Date accomplished:
❐ I will use my tables to record my assertive responses, and I will reward myself for each five assertive responses I make. ❐ ❐ ❐	What I did: Date accomplished:

REFERENCES

American Institute of Stress. (n.d.). *America's number one health problem.* Retrieved April 10, 2009, from http://www.stress.org/Americas.htm.

Braiker, H. B. (1995). *The disease to please.* New York: McGraw-Hill.

Bristol, C. M., & Sherman, H. (1987). *TNT: The power within you.* New York: Prentice Hall.

Dunham, J., & Varma, V. (Eds.). (1998). *Stress in teachers: Past, present, and future.* London: Whurr.

Fensterheim, H., & Baer, J. (1975). *Don't say "yes" when you want to say "no."* New York: Dell.

Friedman, M., & Rosenman, R. H. (1974). *Type-A behavior and your heart.* New York: Knopf.

Friedman, M., & Ulmer, D. (1984). *Treating type A behavior and your heart.* New York: Fawcett.

Helmstetter, S. (1982). *What to say when you talk to yourself.* New York: Pocket Books.

Lakein, A. (1973). *How to get control of your time and your life.* New York: New American Library.

McKay, M., & Davis, M. (1981). *Thoughts & feelings.* Oakland, CA: New Harbinger.

McKay, M., & Rogers, P. (1985). *The anger control workbook.* Oakland, CA: New Harbinger.

Roskies, E. (1987). *Stress management for the healthy type A.* New York: Guilford.

Sapolsky, R. (1998). *Why zebras don't get ulcers.* New York: Freeman.

Seyle, H. (1976). *The stress of life.* New York: Ballantine Books.

Singer, J. (2009). *Mastering anger management.* Dallas, TX: Hypnosis Network.

5

How to Deflect Stressors

Carefully Planned Plus Warp–Speed Techniques

Wherever you intervene in the stress syndrome, you are acting to break the negative feedback loop. Negative thoughts and physical arousal can no longer escalate into painful emotions. And you have taken a major step toward changing your emotional life.

—Dr. Matthew McKay and Dr. Martha Davis (1981)

LEARNING OBJECTIVES

- I will catch myself *awfulizing* and stop it immediately.
- I will continue to recognize the specific negative-thinking patterns I tend to use when I feel disturbing emotions.
- I will practice organizing my thoughts, looking for patterns, and developing rebuttals using the Thinking-Pattern Worksheet (TPW).
- I will use the thought-stopping, calming-breathing, writing-it-down, or worry-time technique every time I catch myself with negative, self-defeating thoughts.

Debbie P. is a third-grade teacher. Her typical week includes dealing with unruly children, unhappy parents, and unbearable workloads. Debbie recalls many evenings when she would come home from school and wonder if she could ever be happy with her job. Overwhelmed, underappreciated, and feeling disjointed from her colleagues, Debbie began to question the passion that led her to teaching. What did Debbie do? As before, we'll discover the answer at the end of the chapter.

Job-related and life stressors are all *invitations* to feel the emotional and physical symptoms of stress. However, as we discovered in Chapter 3, once you recognize the *habitual patterns* of your automatic thinking in your response to those stressors, you have completed the first step in being able to quickly modify those thoughts and eventually avoid thinking that way in the first place. Remember, the stressors and provocations of life are inevitable; how you react to them is a choice over which you have control.

Learning to modify distorted thoughts and quickly replace them with rational, healthy ones forms the foundation for one of the most revolutionary discoveries in the field of mental health and psychotherapy to appear in the past 50 years: Cognitive Behavioral Therapy and the art of Cognitive Stress Intervention.

Earlier, you learned that the stress any individual feels at any time is only about 10% related to recent events in that person's life; but a hefty 90% of that stress is related to one's *internal reaction* to those events. Therefore, the key to both reducing stress once it is felt and preventing further stress lies in your internal self-talk—your interpretation of each event, as you perceive it, through the filter of your specific belief system. Cognitive Behavioral Therapy and Cognitive Stress Intervention are cutting-edge strategies directed at quickly reducing and even preventing stress. In this chapter, you will learn five of these powerful strategies.

RECOGNIZE YOUR THINKING PATTERNS

Adopting the right attitude can convert a negative stress into a positive one.

—Hans Seyle (1976)

As you have already learned, automatic, negative-thinking patterns (e.g., catastrophizing, mind reading, blaming) fuel our internal critic, and it has a field day inviting us to be frightened, stressed, angry, depressed, and so on. Some of the specific characteristics that all automatic thoughts have in common are as follows:

- They are rarely shared with other people. We to talk to ourselves differently than we talk to other people. When we talk to ourselves, we tend to use overgeneralizations, such as, "No one will ever love me," or "I am a complete failure."
- We usually accept these thoughts unquestionably, believing them even though they are irrational. We don't challenge them unless we have been trained to do so (as in this book), and we act as if they *must* be true if those thoughts went through our minds in the first place. Because we don't challenge these thoughts, they are rarely subjected to logical scrutiny.
- They are all learned patterns, and as noted in Chapter 3, we have been told negatives thousands of times while growing up. Often, these thinking patterns are hardwired into us at birth. The patterns then get reinforced and habituated as we hear them from others and repeat them to ourselves.
- They tend to be catastrophic. Automatic thoughts tend to lead to other thoughts, triggering a chain of depressive, frightening, overwhelming, and stressful beliefs, emotions, and behaviors, which can be very difficult to overcome. These thoughts tend to *awfulize* a situation. Such awfulizing usually underlies our experience of anxiety.

Catch yourself whenever you are awfulizing and stop it immediately, using the TPW.

The experience of a negative, painful emotion, such as nervousness, anger, depression, fear, unhappiness, or sadness, is the first clue that you are engaging in distorted, self-defeating self-talk.

| **Figure 5.1** | The A-B-C-D-E Model |

(A) ────► (B) ────► (C) ────► (D) ────► (E)				
Activating event (stress)	Beliefs about the event	Consequent emotions and behaviors (stress)	Disputing thoughts	Energized, revitalized emotions

To review (see Figure 5.1), once you experience unwanted, negative emotions **(C)**, consider those emotions to be a red flag that something

Good News!

Using the TPW as shown in Table 5.1, you can quickly develop healthy thinking habits, replacing the ones that have been destructive to you.

happened **(A)** about which you are talking to yourself negatively **(B)**, and those thoughts need to be examined right now so that you can eventually learn to dispute or rebut them **(D)**. But exactly, how do you examine those thoughts and what do you do about them?

Table 5.1   Debbie's Thinking-Pattern Worksheet (TPW)

Description of the situation (or provocation) that led to her emotional reaction: **(A)**

"I came home from school today, completely drained. Many of my students were unruly and out of control, and I also had to deal with difficult parents."

Debbie's negative emotions **(C)** prior to disputing her thoughts and their intensity (1–10):

1. "I'm feeling overwhelmed."(10)

2. "I'm feeling frightened." (6)

3. "I'm very worried." (8)

Automatic Thoughts and Beliefs (B)	*Self-Defeating Thinking Pattern*	Disputing Responses (Rebuttal) (D)
1. "I had a terrible day at school today, and I'm sure it will be the same every day. This is a disaster!"	*a. Overgeneralization* *b. Magnification*	a. "There is no need to magnify this or blow it out of proportion. Let's not make it worse than it is. First, it doesn't have to be like this every day. I can come up with some ways to interest the children and maintain their attention. In addition, I can cope with this and this is not really a disaster. It may be unfortunate, but that is a lot different than a disaster, and I can rebound from this."

Automatic Thoughts and Beliefs (B)	*Self-Defeating Thinking Pattern*	Disputing Responses (Rebuttal) (D)
2. "I don't think I'm really cut out for this career. I'll never be a successful teacher."	*a. Fortune-telling*	a. "Does this experience really mean that I will never be successful? What are the realistic odds of me not being successful? Are they 90%? Are they 10%? Where is the evidence to support my fear of failure?
3. "I don't know what to do, and my principal is probably going to hear about how I can't control my class, and she will also see me as a failure."	*a. Mind reading*	a. "The principal hired me because she saw something in me that she predicted would make me successful, and success is not simply based on one or two days of experience."
4. "I'll probably be fired."	*a. Fortune-telling*	a. "If the principal is really not disgusted with me, it is unlikely that I'm going to be fired over this."

Negative emotions after rebutting my thoughts and their intensity (1–10):

1. "I'm feeling overwhelmed."(3)
2. "I'm feeling frightened." (1)
3. "I'm very worried." (2)
4. —————————————————————————
5. —————————————————————————

Self-Defeating Thinking Patterns: all or nothing; magnification; mind reading; catastrophizing; being right; should, have to, must; control fallacy; overgeneralization; blaming; emotional reasoning

Adapted from Matthew McKay and Martha Davis. *Thoughts and Feelings.*, 1981, with permission from New Harbinger Press.

THE THINKING-PATTERN WORKSHEET (TPW)

Those who identify with success are welcomed by success; those who identify with failure are likewise welcomed by failure. . . . The words you choose are the seeds of your future realities.

—Lao Tzu, Tao Te Ching

Let's look at Debbie P's situation in Table 5.1, where she comes home mentally exhausted at the end of a day, after dealing with several unruly third graders and complaining parents (A). Debbie feels overwhelmed, frightened, and worried (C). As you learned earlier, if these emotions are left unchecked, they can lead to a host of physical symptoms. It follows, then, that these physical symptoms can lead to absenteeism, which can become habitual because staying away from school obviously avoids the stressors and reduces the physical symptoms that originally came about when she felt stressed.

So if Debbie does not examine her self-talk (B) about her classroom situation (A), she could very well begin to get ill and avoid school—symptoms of burnout.

On the other hand, if Debbie does examine her self-talk, she can determine which thoughts are irrational, distorted, and self-defeating. Using the TPW, as soon as Debbie recognizes that she is experiencing negative emotions, she writes down those emotions and records the strength of each, on a 1-to-10 scale. Second, she records the automatic thoughts that immediately preceded the emotions, and using the list of 10 thinking-pattern distortions at the bottom of the table, she determines what, if any, distorted-thinking patterns were involved. Notice that I said *if any*. This is because we sometimes have negative, automatic thoughts that are realistic and not distorted. For example, if a student hit another student at the end of class, and that student went home crying, it would *not* be a distortion for Debbie to think, "I'm going to hear from that student's parents and will have to explain how this happened." This is the most probable thing that will happen, and it is, therefore, not a distortion. But the vast majority of our negative thinking is distorted and is not based on rational conclusions we have determined. (You can keep a copy of Table 3.3 handy to help you remember the definitions of the distorted-thinking patterns.)

As you can see from Debbie's TPW, after writing down the situation, her emotions, and the automatic thoughts that she can identify, Debbie examines them carefully to see if they represent any distorted-thinking patterns. Notice that her first thought is an example of both blowing things out of proportion and intensifying her feelings and arousal.

Therefore, these thoughts fall into the patterns of *overgeneralization* and *magnification.*

Her second thought is an example of predicting a negative outcome in the future, without really giving her a chance to explore the possibilities (*fortune-telling* or *catastrophizing*).

As Debbie predicts what her principal is likely to do, she is engaging in *fortune-telling*, and then assuming the principal will see her as a failure, Debbie is engaging in the *mind reading* distortion.

Finally, fearing that she will be fired is another example of the catastrophic-thinking pattern of *fortune-telling*.

Once Debbie recognizes the distorted, self-defeating thinking patterns that led to the emotions in the first place, it's time to use her creative-thinking skills to come up with rational rebuttals to each of the distorted thoughts **(D)**.

The next time you feel any negative emotion (e.g., overwhelmed, frightened, depressed, irritated, impatient, hopeless), do the following: Use the TPW and describe the event that led to the emotions; write down the specific emotions you feel and rate them. Write down the automatic thoughts that preceded you feeling those emotions, and determine which distortion patterns those thoughts fit. Then write down rebuttal thoughts that make sense. Believing those rebuttal thoughts should help you feel better.

In Table 5.1, you see examples of the rebuttal thoughts that Debbie came up with. So once Debbie realized that her automatic-thinking patterns in the first column are examples of overgeneralization and magnification, she considered alternative thoughts that are not self-defeating. For example, instead of telling herself that her school experience is a disaster, Debbie can see that this is an example of magnification. She can think of different ways of treating her students that may result in less disruption, and she certainly does not need to interpret what's happening as a *disaster!*

With her second thought, Debbie recognizes that she is magnifying her fears of success way out of proportion. She asks herself the logical question of "Where is the evidence that these unfortunate experiences mean that I will never succeed?" Perhaps she can brainstorm solutions to her problems with her teaching colleagues.

Debbie's rebuttal thoughts about how the principal will most likely *not be* disgusted with her are very logical and appropriate. Obviously, this rebuttal then makes the idea that she will inevitably be fired a silly assumption, which also needs to be eliminated from her thinking. Once all of these negative thoughts are rebutted, she reexamines her emotions and rates their strength again. When you are doing this for yourself, if you have been honest and have written rebuttals that you really believe in, those emotions either will disappear altogether or will be dramatically reduced in their intensity.

This TPW technique is awkward at first because you are not used to writing down your thoughts, but if you will take the time to write down your automatic thoughts whenever you are feeling a negative emotion, and then simply look through the list of distorted-thinking patterns at the bottom of the table to see if your thoughts fit one of those categories, most of the time, you will find that there is at least one distortion that you are using in your thinking. You can then use all of your creative energies to come up with rebuttals that logically dispute the original thoughts, and these rebuttals are based on logic and evidence. You will then find that your negative feelings will dissolve, as you recognize that your new thoughts make more sense than the original ones. This is the best way to overcome the *internal critic* and keep it from controlling you!

Are you ready to try this method for yourself? First, keep an original and make copies of the TPW in Table 5.2 so you have them for any future situations that may arise.

To practice, use one of the copies, and think of a recent situation (**A**) where you felt a strong, negative emotion, such as anger, frustration, sadness, anxiety, or panic. Write down the situation, the specific emotions you felt (**C**), and the strength of each emotion, from 1 to 10. Next, list as many automatic thoughts and beliefs that you can recall that went through your mind before you noticed those emotions (**B**). Now, look back at the list of negative thinking patterns from the bottom of the TPW, or from Table 3.3, and see which ones fit your particular thoughts. Finally, write down disputing (rebuttal) thoughts (**D**), using the examples given in Table 5.1. Think carefully here because coming up with rational rebuttal statements will always help you to defuse your negative emotions about a situation. Finally, reexamine your original emotions and rate their intensity once again. Notice the difference?

If you use the TPW whenever you are feeling strong, negative emotions, it will pay handsome dividends in terms of changing your mood and stress level.

Keep practicing this exercise and you will soon learn how to deflect the stress that comes from these unchecked thoughts automatically, in your head. You will graduate from using the form to giving yourself instant rebuttal thoughts in your head at warp-speed!

When you don't have time to use the TPW, use the thought-stopping, calming-breathing, write-it-down, or worry-time techniques described next.

Table 5.2	My Thinking-Pattern Worksheet (TPW)

Make copies of this table before you fill it in so you can use it every time you feel stressed.

Description of the situation that led to my emotional reaction **(A)**:

Negative emotions **(C)** prior to rebutting my thoughts and their intensity (1–10):

1. ——————————————————————————————
2. ——————————————————————————————
3. ——————————————————————————————

Automatic Thoughts and Beliefs (B)	*Self-Defeating Thinking Pattern*	Disputing Responses (Rebuttal) (D)
1.	*a.* *b.*	1.
2.	*a.* *b.*	2.
3.	*a.* *b.*	3.
4.	*a.* *b.*	4.

If you have more than four thoughts, continue this on another sheet.

Negative emotions after rebutting my thoughts and their intensity 1–10:

1. ——————————————————————————————
2. ——————————————————————————————
3. ——————————————————————————————
4. ——————————————————————————————
5. ——————————————————————————————

Self-Defeating Thinking Patterns: all or nothing; magnification; mind reading; catastrophizing; being right; should, have to, must; control fallacy; overgeneralization; blaming; emotional reasoning

Adapted from Matthew McKay and Martha Davis. *Thoughts and Feelings.*, 1981, with permission from New Harbinger Press.

A THOUGHT-STOPPING TECHNIQUE

Thoughts repeated become believed. Thoughts believed become reality.

—Unknown

Obviously, there are many times when you are teaching, driving, or in a store and you cannot easily write down the negative thoughts that you realize are occurring at that moment. In situations like that, you can employ a rapid method for stopping these thoughts in their tracks, without the necessity of using a TPW to analyze the cause of your emotional reactions.

Here is a technique I have used with clients for more than 30 years, and it really works (Mahoney, 1971). Get a thick, Number 64 rubber band that is used to wrap bundles of your mail. Write a positive thought on the rubber band, such as, "Just relax, this will pass," and associate this positive thought with the rubber band. Wear the rubber band on your wrist.

The second purpose of the rubber band is the most important. Whenever you recognize thoughts are distorted and making you feel bad, pull back on the band, snap it on your wrist, and at the same time, in your head, shout, "Stop this silly thinking!" Once the thought stops, immediately take a couple of deep breaths in through your nose and out through your mouth, relaxing your body and telling yourself a disputing positive thought.

As an example, let's say you're in the middle of your school day, and you feel angry and irritable. When you have time for a break, you stop and think about what you were just thinking. "My principal doesn't really give two cents about me and my children who are defiant and oppositional. I'm on my own here." This is the time to snap the rubber band, take a series of deep breaths, and as you exhale and calm down, tell yourself, "My principal has to spread her attention to many teachers and each has important issues. Eventually, she will get around to me. I just need to keep on her radar screen."

A CALMING-BREATHING TECHNIQUE

As you recall from Chapter 1, when we feel provoked, we switch on the sympathetic nervous system (SNS), which includes rapid breathing. The important thing to remember is that rapid breathing is necessary for dealing with real emergencies because we need to rapidly transmit oxygen to our brains to make quick decisions. But when we switch on the SNS because of our negative internal dialogue, there is no real emergency and, therefore, no need for rapid breathing. In fact, such rapid breathing is usually shallow (only the chest and shoulders move) breathing, which can increase the tension and discomfort you feel. So one of the best things we can do whenever we feel strain and upsetting emotions is to practice a *calming*-breathing technique, where you get a full volume of air, beginning in your abdomen and moving up. Here it is:

Fold your hands over your stomach area, and take slow, deep breaths in through your nose and out through your mouth. Are your hands moving out as you breathe in and moving back in as you exhale? If not, practice, over and over, as if you are filling a glass from the bottom up. Close your eyes and imagine that there is a balloon inside your abdomen. Each time you inhale, imagine the balloon filling with air.

Every time you are sitting or reclining, practice this type of breathing by folding your hands over your stomach. Once you find your hands moving as you inhale and exhale, you've mastered it! Practice every day until this becomes part of your natural breathing style.

WRITE-IT-DOWN TECHNIQUE

Set a time, several times a week, when you will write down your feelings and thoughts. Putting your feelings into words that you can read helps you sort out the rational from irrational ones. It also gives you a sense of release.

Make a specific schedule for your writing time. For example, you may want to spend 10 or 15 minutes writing down your feelings and thoughts about your day just before retiring for the evening. Be sure that this writing place is one where you won't be interrupted or disturbed. Perhaps reserve a private file on your computer for this daily writing. You don't need to share the writings with anyone, so you can feel free to explore your very deepest thoughts and feelings.

Just freely write down what comes into your mind, without worrying about grammar, spelling, or the like. This can be a really cathartic experience for you. If writing seems too much of a chore, record your thoughts and feelings into a recorder. Just saying them aloud will help calm you.

WORRY-TIME TECHNIQUE

Many people worry throughout the day, constantly setting off their SNS, resulting in mood and stress fluctuations that fill their days. This simple technique really works to prevent this: Choose a *worry time* of a maximum of 10 minutes each day. Save up all of your worries and think about them only during this 10-minute time period. Try to use a "safe time," such as just when you get home from school, rather than right before going to bed. Realize that constant worrying accomplishes nothing positive, so why not just cram it all into this 10-minute worry time, and then free yourself all through the rest of your waking day? The key to this method is to force yourself to only worry during this worry time. If worries enter your mind after your worry time, stop them in their tracks and tell yourself that you will save them for the next day's worry time.

MAKE A CONTRACT WITH YOURSELF

Reward yourself for successfully warding off worry and stress using the techniques listed in this chapter. Do a pleasant activity as a reward (e.g., go to a bookstore or coffee shop). You can even make morning activities that you must do (e.g., brush your teeth, comb your hair) contingent on completion of one of the Stress Mastery Prescriptions listed in this chapter and throughout the book. Write out the contract for yourself on your computer and keep it on your screen.

When you stick to such a contract, there is a great incentive to practice your new stress-mastery skills because you *have to* brush your teeth and comb your hair before you leave for school in the morning. Always do the thing you are procrastinating *first*. Don't fool yourself into thinking, "I'll do it right after I comb my hair."

So what happened to Debbie P.? Recall that she was feeling overwhelmed in her elementary school teaching role because of unruly students, difficult parents, and feeling disjointed from her colleagues.

Debbie was fortunate that she was working in a school where brainstorming sessions with all of the teachers and the administrators were regularly scheduled events. Each morning before school started, the teachers shared ideas for dealing with discipline problems, unhappy parents, and any other problem. They clarified issues so that none of the teachers would assume that the stressors they were dealing with were impossible to overcome. They helped one another recognize when they were exaggerating the situations and how their distorted thoughts were causing much of their distress.

Once the emotions calmed down, ideas began to flow, and Debbie instituted them in her class. She had fun contests. For example, "grabbers for good behavior" was a prize-based, behavior-modification program she instituted in her class, with much success. With the principal setting the tone, the faculty and administrators had frequent out of school get-togethers with their families, such as picnics, progressive dinners, and theme parties.

Inservice programs were conducted as retreats, away from the school. All of the teachers began to know one another and their families, and they developed a strong support system of colleagues.

Instead of feeling overwhelmed and hopeless, Debbie began to feel in control of both her class and her emotions. And when she had those dreary days, she would come home and write down her feelings and thoughts. She also made it a habit to remember those special moments when she received letters or personal visits from past students who told Debbie how she had a profound impact on their lives and how much they appreciated her.

ACTION PLAN FOR STRESS MASTERY

Table 5.3	Action Plan for Stress Mastery

Check off when completed.	
New Behavior	*What I Did and the Date Accomplished*
☐ I will catch myself awfulizing and stop it immediately. ☐ ☐ ☐	What I did: Date accomplished:
☐ Every day I will continue to recognize the specific negative-thinking patterns I tend to use when I feel disturbing emotions. ☐ ☐ ☐	What I did: Date accomplished:
☐ I will practice organizing my thoughts, looking for patterns, and developing rebuttals using the Thinking-Pattern Worksheet (TPW). ☐ ☐ ☐	What I did: Date accomplished:
☐ I will use the thought-stopping, calming-breathing, writing-it-down, make a contract, and worry-time techniques every time I catch myself with negative moods or emotions. ☐ ☐ ☐	What I did: Date accomplished:

REFERENCES

Beck, A. T., & Emory, G. (1986). *Anxiety disorders and phobias.* New York: Basic Books.

Mahoney, M. J. (1971). The self-management of covert behavior: A case study. *Behavior Therapy, 2,* 575–578.

McKay, M., & Davis, M. (1981). *Thoughts & feelings.* Oakland, CA: New Harbinger.

Seyle, H. (1976). *The stress of life.* New York: Ballantine Books.

Shelton, J. L., & Levy, R. L. (1981). *Behavioral assignments and treatment compliance.* Champaign, IL: Research Press.

Singer, J. (2006). Interview with Dr. Jack Singer. In D. Wright (Ed.), *Dynamic health* (pp. 1–15). Sevierville, TN: Insight.

Singer, J. N. (1995). Conquering your internal critic so you can sing your own song. In D. M. Walters (Ed.), *Great speakers anthology,* (Vol. 4, pp. 160–195). Glendora, CA: Royal.

PART II

Prescriptions for Building Your Psychological Immunity to Stress

6

How to Harness the Power Within and Inoculate Yourself Against the Impact of Inevitable Stressors

What lies behind us and what lies before us are tiny matters compared to what lies within us.

—Oliver Wendell Holmes, author and poet

LEARNING OBJECTIVES

- I will become aware of my thinking patterns that provoke stress.
- I will learn the three Cs of stress hardiness and tips for building *commitment*, *control*, and *challenge*.
- I will learn how to use the components of self-efficacy to buffer myself against stress.

(Continued)

(Continued)

- I will learn how to use the power of goal setting to increase my stress hardiness.
- I will understand the eight questions to ask myself regarding each goal I set.
- I will learn how to use the power of *positive affirmations* to enhance my hardiness.

In this chapter, I am deviating from using an example of a teacher's success over stress to make the point of the chapter. Instead, I will describe my own stress, as I am facing fast-approaching deadlines from my publisher. I find myself procrastinating, finding all sorts of excuses to avoid sitting down at my computer. I have had no shortage of reasons to avoid writing. For example, because I am running a private practice and a professional speaking career simultaneously with writing this book, I constantly need to prepare for the patients I am seeing on any particular day and new ideas for polishing my speeches constantly enter my mind, pulling me away from my writing.

Despite the fact that I am a stress-mastery expert, I have to be constantly vigilant to stress symptoms, analyzing my self-talk and rebutting negative thoughts, such as, "What if I don't make the deadlines?" Part of my introspective analysis has led me to the conclusion that I am very compulsive about putting every piece of relevant information that I find into my book. Consequently, I constantly bombard myself with *what-if-I-missed-something* thoughts, which usually lead to me putting the writing aside so that I won't have to deal with those what-if concerns. Obviously, it's critical to understand my own negative thinking patterns so that I don't develop excessive stress and avoidance of the task. Read on to learn what I did to overcome these self-defeating habits, based on the stress-inoculation techniques presented in this chapter.

HOW TO BEGIN THE INOCULATION PROCESS

What your eyes see and your ears hear, if seen and heard often enough, you remember . . . and make a part of your life.

—Claude Bristol (1987)

Just as being inoculated against diseases builds our resilience and protects us from those diseases, *psychological inoculation* means developing skills to help you resist stressors and build your resistance to their impact.

Resilience to stress begins with repetition of *positive* thoughts, beliefs, and images. Doing this will begin to change your attitude and confidence. As I am so fond of saying, your dreams have no barriers, and the only difference between your dreams and your reality is the presence of your internal critic and the resultant lack of confidence.

HOW TO BUILD RESILIENCE TO STRESS: THE THREE CS OF STRESS HARDINESS

In the middle of every difficulty lies an opportunity.

—Albert Einstein

In Chapter 4, you learned about two types of personalities that are most prone to stress unless the people with those traits become aware of them and focus on changing their habitual responses to provocations.

Indeed, there are also some folks who fortunately are hardwired with stress-*resistant* traits. Maddi (2002, 2006) coined the term *stress hardiness* to refer to these people. But just as those genetically predisposed with stress-prone personalities can learn to change their behaviors, people can learn to develop stress-resistant traits, even if they weren't born stress-hardy. This hardiness is made up of three components: *commitment*, *control*, and *challenge*. Together, these three components empower people to become resilient, despite experiencing the inevitable provocations and stressors of life (Khoshaba & Maddi, 1999; Maddi, 2002).

> **Good News!**
>
> Even if you were not born hardwired with the three Cs (which many astronauts and test pilots are, for example), you can *learn* to develop these characteristics as adults. The result is that you will thrive, even in the face of highly stressful provocations. This is the difference between the teacher who gets overwhelmed and the one who thrives under virtually the same stress-provoking situations.

1. Commitment

You decided to become a teacher because of your personal vision and purpose in life. You dedicated your educational goals to making a real difference in the lives of children. Ask yourself if your actual work as a teacher has relevance to your long-term goals. Most likely, the answer is yes. Individuals who are committed to both short- and long-term goals, and *stay committed* regardless of unfortunate events and the resultant negative thoughts that creep into their minds, are the most successful people. Committed teachers see the real value in staying involved in their jobs and close to their support systems, even when the stress mounts (Maddi, 2008).

Teachers who possess *or develop* this trait are committed to their work and stay focused on the value they are providing their students, regardless of the feedback they do, or do not, receive. They believe the particular contribution they are making to the lives of their students really matters. A teacher friend of mine, Brenda H., recently told me that one of the highlights of her career took place when one of her second-grade pupils appeared in her classroom years later, after getting her teaching credentials. She told Brenda that she was the inspiration for her choosing that noble career! Whether you receive this feedback or not, you are touching people's lives in positive ways with each year you teach!

Commit yourself to a few years at a time, and pour all of your energy into that relatively short commitment. At the end of the time frame, you can make a decision as to whether you want to recommit or leave the profession. But by committing to a specific time frame, you won't risk feeling overwhelmed or burned out. You might be surprised at how devoted you will become when there is a reasonable reconsideration time built into your life plan.

Engaging more deeply in working relationships with your teaching colleagues and administrators will help you to commit and feel like an integral part of the educational process.

2. Control

Stress-hardy teachers are *inner* directed, meaning that they believe they are in control of their own destiny. They enjoy being able to make decisions related to their work, as opposed to being micromanaged by supervisors.

Stress-hardy people look at stressors as motivators for them to turn the stressors to their advantage and even gain more control. They keep trying to influence outcomes, rather than feeling powerless (Maddi, 2008).

Join committees that have genuine impact on decisions made in your school. If this is not available, volunteer your time and get involved in those activities resulting in the implementation of important decisions. Again, a strong working relationship with your colleagues can buffer you against job stressors over which you feel little control.

3. Challenge

Stress-hardy people see stress as part of life, and they see such challenges as opportunities to learn how to grow, *despite* the stress. They aren't rattled when their comfort is disrupted (Maddi, 2008).

Life is full of obstacles. When I accepted the assignment of writing this book, I gave myself a series of deadlines. The easiest thing to do would have been to look at this task as overwhelming and too difficult to accomplish. I could have begged off the assignment and given myself more time so that I could do the other things that I love to do. However, this would be giving in to my internal critic, forcing me to procrastinate because of fear that I would not be able to accomplish the task on time.

Instead, I forced myself to look at this as a *challenge* and continued to focus on how wonderful I would feel once I had completed the task. Successful people consistently look at obstacles as challenges, as opposed to being overwhelmed by those obstacles. Feeling overwhelmed leads to more negative thinking, ultimately leading to procrastination to avoid the anticipated failure.

Teachers who learn to be stress-hardy view obstacles as challenges, not as insurmountable roadblocks. They thrive on overcoming their challenges, rather than giving up. So continually remind yourself about how the work you're doing with your students adds to your personal vision and purpose in life. Look for resources to help you overcome those challenges, such as the guidelines described next.

The Critical Challenges of Keeping Order in the Classroom

Let's look at one of the most stressful aspects of your job as a teacher, regardless of what grade level you teach: classroom management. As Rebecca Clay (2009) says it, "Put simply, K–12 teachers don't always get the training

> **Good News!**
>
> One of the biggest challenges you will face in teaching is maintaining order in your classroom. You can master this challenge by using the powerful resources that are found in Resource D.

they need to handle disruptive behavior in their classrooms" (p. 64). This is a particular problem for new, inexperienced teachers and represents one of the main reasons for teacher burnout and turnover, regardless of years of experience.

The stress-hardy teacher sees these provocations as obstacles that have solutions, rather than being overwhelmed by them and feeling helpless. They know that there are resources available to solve these problems. For example, the American Psychological Association's Center for Psychology in Schools and Education (APA, CPSE) provides a wealth of research-based advice on critical subjects, including how to motivate students, deal with bullies, and manage a classroom (APA, 2009).

Resource D provides specific Web sites that the CPSE recommends for help managing disruptive behavior in the classroom (APA, 2008). These techniques follow a three-tiered model of:

1. promoting a positive environment in the classroom,

2. addressing and predicting children at risk for disruptive behavior, and

3. targeting and managing students who have already disrupted their classrooms.

Armed with this information, you can now look at the stressors of classroom disruptions as *challenges,* rather than as obstacles, for which you now have the exact resources to deal with them effectively.

HOW TO BUILD A SENSE OF SELF-EFFICACY

Our research shows that teacher self-efficacy might act as a physiological toughening agent. Self-efficacy might constitute a health-protective resource in teachers.

—Schwerdtfeger, Konermann, and Schönhofen (2008)

There is new and exciting research about teachers (Schwerdtfeger et al., 2008) that shows much promise for helping to build stress hardiness. Teachers who face job-related obstacles and setbacks and then can convince themselves that they have what it takes to master these challenges develop not only stress hardiness, but also physical hardiness, as barriers to stress. Perceived self-efficacy is the confident belief that you really have the capability to accomplish what you wish in your teaching career, regardless of the challenges inherent in the job. This strong, confident belief system includes the belief that you definitely have choices over your responses to events that affect your life. Obviously, what you have learned in Part I of this book will contribute to this belief.

People with a strong sense of self-efficacy quickly recover their confidence after failures or setbacks, and they attribute those setbacks to lack of knowledge, skills, or effort on their part—all of which they can control by recognizing such deficiencies and working on them. So you can see that, for these people, their sense of control over circumstances in their lives is reinforced.

Teachers high in self-efficacy exhibit lower stress hormones and fewer cardiac complaints (Schwerdtfeger et al., 2008). The results of these studies are compatible with the view that teacher self-efficacy might act as a physiological toughening agent.

Rx 37
Stress Mastery

Don't try to control that which cannot be controlled or things that have already happened. Stick with what you are capable of controlling in the present.

Of course, there are direct parallels between self-efficacy beliefs, taking control of your internal critic, the three Cs of hardiness, and goal setting, which you will learn about later in this chapter.

Table 6.1 gives examples of positive thoughts that lead to these remarkable outcomes for teachers. I have left spaces for you to fill in additional positive statements about yourself.

Table 6.1	Examples of Self-Efficacy Thoughts

Add your own thoughts in the spaces provided.

1. "When I give it careful thought and effort, I am able to reach even the most difficult students."

1a. ————————————————————————————

1b. ————————————————————————————

2. "I am convinced that, with more experience, I will continue to become more and more capable of helping address my students' needs."

2a. ————————————————————————————

2b. ————————————————————————————

3. "I know that I can maintain a positive relationship with parents, even when tensions arise."

3a. ————————————————————————————

3b. ————————————————————————————

4. "I am sure that I can develop creative ways to cope with administrative constraints (such as budget cuts, new curriculum demands, and testing requirements) and continue to thrive in my teaching role."

4a. ————————————————————————————

4b. ————————————————————————————

To develop stress hardiness and self-efficacy, you must believe in yourself and understand that *you* have the ultimate control over what your thoughts and beliefs will be.

Good News!

There are many additional ways to develop a sense of stress hardiness and self-efficacy. Table 6.2 provides some proven ideas.

There are habits that can help you develop the attitudes of commitment, control, challenge, and overall self-efficacy. Two of them are to focus on attainable goals and use the power of positive affirmations.

Table 6.2	How to Develop Stress Hardiness and Self-Efficacy

1. Study colleagues who seem to be very resilient to the stressors at school. Try to learn how they cope or manage those stressors. Watching a colleague, who is similar to you, in a similar situation, yet more successful, will help convince you that you too possess the capabilities to master comparable challenges at school.

2. Make a list of colleagues who are *deficient* in attitudes of stress hardiness, and study how they deal with similar stressors. Obviously, you'll want to make sure you don't model their behavior and start modeling the behavior of the resilient folks.

3. Focus on each successful accomplishment you have. Successes build the belief that you can master such problems in the future. Pay attention to the people around you who build you up and tell you that you have what it takes. Continually give yourself positive feedback, and focus on feedback from others who recognize what you're doing and feedback from your students, parents, and colleagues who ultimately benefit from what you have done.

4. When times are tough in school, stick to your plan. You will emerge much stronger by working through this adversity.

5. Always look for the silver lining in every dark cloud you face in your job.

6. Always look at stress-provoking situations in your job as *opportunities* to use your abilities to solve those problems.

HOW TO USE THE POWER OF GOAL SETTING TO STAY FOCUSED DESPITE STRESS PROVOCATIONS

With goals, you become what you want. Without them, you remain what you were.

—Lee Pulos (2004)

Research cited by Dr. David Burns (1989) shows that you are approximately 11 times more likely to follow through on goals if you write them down and regularly revisit them, as opposed to just thinking about them in your head.

Realistic goal setting helps remove helpless feelings, creates a positive future, breathes life into that future, and helps you to visualize that future. Successful people are willing to transform themselves, change, and grow, and goal setting helps accomplish those ends. For example, elite athletes can recite the series of goals that they set for themselves to get to the top of their sport. But we sometimes unconsciously sabotage ourselves in the quest to accomplish our goals.

Rx 38
Stress
Mastery

*Make a list of your short- and long-term goals, **right now**, and answer the eight questions listed in Table 6.3 for each goal.*

Table 6.3 is a list of eight questions to ask yourself about each goal. These questions will help you define your goal and realize how you have been undermining yourself in the past. Use a separate sheet of paper (or file on the computer) for each goal you have, and be sure to write your responses to these eight questions for each goal you have.

Table 6.3   Questions to Ask Yourself Regarding Each Goal

My Questions	*My Answers*
Write down your goal:	
1. Why do I want to accomplish this goal?	1.
2. What are three things that will happen to let me know that I have accomplished this goal?	2.
3. What will I hear others say that will let me know that I have achieved my goal?	3.
4. What kinds of things will I say to myself once I have achieved my goal?	4.
5. What feelings/emotions will I be experiencing on attainment of my goal?	5.
6. How can I sabotage myself in my quest for this goal?	6.

(Continued)

| Table 6.3 | (Continued) |

My Questions	My Answers
7. What quality(s) do I need to develop in myself to achieve my goal?	7.
8. What small gesture or step can I make to act as if I'm already on my way toward accomplishing my goal?	8.

Read your goals aloud to yourself 10 times *each day*. Don't put this off. *Today* is your point of power, where you can create the optimal future for yourself. So when you focus on future goals, and imagine them becoming a reality soon, you are able to release all of the obstacles that have held you back from accomplishing these goals before. In short, release the past (failures to achieve) and imagine each goal taking place *now*.

THE POWER OF DESIRE, IMAGINATION, AND EXPECTATION

When you set realistic goals for yourself and you're serious about accomplishing them, you're releasing a "slumbering giant" of potential, which has been residing within, waiting to express itself. This represents all of the latent talent and creativity you have kept locked up inside because of your self-doubt and your internal belief that your fate in life was sealed years ago. You can throw off the shackles of self-doubt, fear, and intimidation by sustaining your desire to attain your goals, expecting that you will achieve them, and using your imagination to visualize yourself as you will be once you attain those goals.

So when you write down your goals, keep in mind that you need to have the fire and passion to accomplish them **(desire)**, rather than targeting these goals because someone else in your life has decided that you should work on them. When you lie down to retire each evening, just when you are in that sleepy state between awake and asleep, visualize (**imagination**) yourself as if you have already accomplished your goals and feel all of the happy emotions connected with that vision as if this is your reality today. Act as if what you want has already happened. This brings the future into the present.

Finally, anticipate (**expectation**) that you will succeed. Nothing awakens the slumbering giant as much as expecting success. Releasing these three keys is a continual process that you can practice each day. Try it—you'll be amazed at the results.

People who worry about situations over which they will never have control cannot easily develop the three Cs, and they ultimately lose faith in their ability to achieve their goals. Accordingly, regardless of the lack of positive feedback you receive from others, *each day* you should reflect on your accomplishments and achievements and give yourself a pat on the back. One way to make this happen much easier is by using positive affirmations.

HOW TO USE THE POWER OF POSITIVE AFFIRMATIONS TO DEVELOP THE THREE CS AND ACCOMPLISH YOUR GOALS

Thoughts of your mind have made you what you are, and thoughts of your mind will make you what you become from this day forward.

—Catherine Ponder, author

Positive affirmations are nothing more than specific, positive statements that you make to yourself. The problem is that most people more often have negative thoughts about themselves and their lives, rather than positive affirmations, running through their minds.

Affirmations can be written on 3×5 cards, on your computer desktop, or, ideally, recorded so you can listen to your voice uttering them over and over.

For maximum effectiveness, Fishel (2003) recommends that each affirmation must be:

1. positive;

2. uttered with gusto, power, and conviction;

3. said in the here and now (present);

4. possible to attain; and

5. only about you, not others.

To develop attitudes of hardiness, and to stick to your goals, start using positive affirmations daily. Write down or record your affirmations and read or listen to them at least 10 times a day for a minimum of 21 days.

"Countless experiments have proven that change occurs within 21 days when we repeat our affirmation at least ten times each day" (Fishel, 2003, p. 18). The key to this dramatic finding is repeating the affirmation(s) at least ten times each day, for 21 *consecutive* days.

As you now know, the sympathetic nervous system goes into emergency mode whenever we even *think* about something that concerns us, so our subconscious mind doesn't know the difference between a real threat and one that is imagined through our self-talk. Think about and visualize going to your high school or college reunion and spotting a dear friend you haven't seen in years. Now, close your eyes and try to visualize that moment actually happening. Do you feel an instant chill or warm feeling coming over you?

Now think about cuddling your pet or sitting on a beach with a gentle breeze in your hair, watching a marvelous sunset. How do these thoughts and images make you feel physically? You can see that your thoughts bring about images, and those images rapidly lead to physical changes in your body. As Ruth Fishel (2003) says, "Words can block us from success or bring us success" (p. 10).

In Chapters 3 and 5, you learned how to recognize typical negative-thinking patterns in which you frequently engage and how to stop them. Now, you can go beyond that to develop *positive* thoughts (affirmations), which can become habits that are part of your daily life; think these thoughts when you are getting dressed, on the way to school, during breaks in your workday, on your way home, and before you retire for the evening.

As with your goals, you can use several reminders for your affirmations. Keep a separate notebook to write down your affirmations, type them on the computer, have a computer reminder bring them up on your desktop each day, have sticky notes on the frame of your computer screen to remind you to write them down each day, and record them into a cassette or digital recorder so you can actually hear them in your own voice several times a day.

You can use your creativity and your own specific needs to create your affirmations. However, here are some examples, by category, to give you a jump start.

Commitment

- "I am committed to reviewing this book weekly to build my resilience to stress."
- "I am committed to observing others whom I admire and modeling their successful behavior."

- "I am committed to staying at my job and making a difference in the lives of students, despite the obstacles I face."

Control

- "I am ultimately in control of my mind and body."
- "I recognize my internal critic, and I know how to control it."
- "I know what I can control and what I cannot. I only focus on what I can control."

Challenge

- "I look at stress-provoking situations on my job as opportunities to use my untapped abilities to solve them."
- "I thrive on challenges, as my ability to creatively solve those challenges flows easily and effortlessly."
- "I embrace obstacles as challenges and challenges as opportunities to succeed."

Goals

- "I set realistic and challenging goals, write them down, and review them every day."
- "My goals are specific. The more specific they are, the easier it is for me to visualize myself accomplishing them."
- "I am passionate about my goals, and I expect to accomplish them."

Change

- "I see every change in my job or responsibilities as a new opportunity to achieve my goals."
- "I know what I can change and what I cannot. I only focus on what I can change."
- "I recognize what I would like to change in my life, and I will focus on that every day."

Confidence

- "I am confident in my ability to overcome obstacles today."
- "I am learning to trust my own wisdom, creativity, and intelligence and give myself permission to take realistic risks in my life."
- "My confidence is growing daily."

Believing in Myself

- "If I ever had any doubts about myself in the past, today is a great day to cast them aside and throw away any disbelief that has ever held me back."

- "I know that my success is 100% up to me. I am a winner because I now know how to look at events in my life and what to do about them."
- "I will stand up for myself, believe in myself, and succeed in whatever I wish. I know I can do it. I am focused and confident."

By now, you probably realize that the action plan at the end of each chapter is actually a set of positive affirmations, so you have a whole list of them already prepared for you to practice.

So what happened to good old Dr. Jack and his procrastination? Well, obviously, I did finish this book, and it was published. I wrote down my goals every day on the computer and read them aloud 10 times each day. In expressing my goals, they were essentially positive affirmations about how I would finish the book, and I visualized feeling wonderful and having teachers from all over the country praising its value. My affirmations were all about my challenge, my feelings of control, and my commitment to finishing this project on time.

I am convinced that if I had not written and reviewed my goals and repeated my positive affirmations each day, then I would have continued procrastinating, and this book may never have made it to publication.

ACTION PLAN FOR STRESS MASTERY

Table 6.4	My Action Plan for Stress Mastery

Check off when completed.	
New Behavior	*What I Did and the Date Accomplished*
❏ Every day I will watch for specific stress-provoking thoughts and stop them immediately, using the rubber-band technique. ❏ ❏ ❏	What I did: Date accomplished:
❏ I will use the tips I learned in Table 6.2 to develop my attitudes of commitment, control, and challenge. ❏ ❏ ❏	What I did: Date accomplished:

New Behavior	What I Did and the Date Accomplished
❏ I will write down or record short- and long-term goals and review them daily. I will affirm each of my goals aloud 10 times a day. ❏ ❏ ❏	What I did: Date accomplished:
❏ For each goal that I write down, I will ask myself the eight key questions and write down the answers. ❏ ❏ ❏	What I did: Date accomplished:
❏ I will make a list of positive affirmations, look at them each day, recite them aloud at least 10 times each day, re-write them and/or record them and listen to them in my own voice each day. ❏ ❏ ❏	What I did: Date accomplished:

REFERENCES

American Psychological Association's Center for Psychology in Schools and Education (APA, CPSE). (2009, January 29). *Applying psychological science to teaching and learning in schools.* Retrieved February 27, 2009, from http://www.apa.org/ed/cpse/.

American Psychological Association's (APA) Coalition of Psychology for Schools and Education. (2008). *Resources on classroom management,* (Appendix A, pp. 1–4). Retrieved February 27, 2009, from http://www.apa.org/ed/cpse/management-appendices.pdf.

Bandura, A. (1994). Self-efficacy. In V. S. Ramachaudran (Ed.), *Encyclopedia of human behavior* (Vol. 4, pp. 71–81). New York: Academic Press.

Bristol, C. M., & Sherman, H. (1987). *TNT: The power within you.* New York: Prentice Hall.

Burns, D. (1989). *The feeling good handbook.* New York: William Morrow.

Clay, R. A. (2009, Fall).Order in the classroom! *Monitor on Psychology, 40*(2), 64.

Fishel, R. (2003). *Change almost anything in 21 days: Recharge your life with the power of over 500 affirmations.* Deerfield Beach, FL: Health Communications.

Helmstetter, S. (1987). *The self-talk solution.* New York: Pocket Books.

Maddi, S. R. (2002). The story of hardiness: Twenty years of theorizing, research, and practice. *Consulting Psychology Journal, 54*, 173–185.

Maddi, S. R. (2006). Hardiness: The courage to be resilient. In J. C. Thomas, D. L. Segal, & M. Herson (Eds.), *Comprehensive handbook of personality and psychopathology: Personality and everyday functioning* (Vol. 1, pp. 306–321). Hoboken, NJ: Wiley.

Maddi, S. R. (2008). The courage and strategies of hardiness as helpful in growing despite major, disruptive stresses. *American Psychologist, 63*(6), 563–564.

Maddi, S. R., & Khoshaba, D. M. (2005). *Resilience at work.* New York: Amacom.

Khoshaba, D. M., & Maddi, S. R. (1999). *Hardiness training: Managing stressful change.* Newport Beach, CA: Hardiness Institute.

Pulos, L. (2004, March). *Sports psychology and performance enhancement.* Paper presented at a meeting of the American Society of Clinical Hypnosis, Denver, CO.

Schwerdtfeger, A., Konermann, L., & Schönhofen, K. (2008). Self-efficacy as a health-protective resource in teachers? A biopsychological approach. *Health Psychology, 27*(3), 358–368.

7

How Fun and Laughter Can Inoculate You: Jest *for the* Health *of It!*

There ain't much fun in medicine, but there's a heck of a lot of medicine in fun.

—Josh Billings, humorist, poet, and lecturer

LEARNING OBJECTIVES

- I will be able to cite the health benefits of adding humor and laughter to my life.
- I will learn how to deal effectively with embarrassing situations that I experience.
- I will learn how to bring fun and humor into my classroom and curriculum.
- I will be able to bring fun and humor to my staff and administration.
- I will be able to bring more fun and humor into my life.

R ich M. has been teaching music and band in middle school for 42 years, and he can't bear the thought of retirement. He swears that in his 42 years, he has *never* had a student talk back to him, and he has *never* had to send a student to the principal. Certainly, Rich has been exposed to the same stressors that most teachers have to deal with, along with some personal medical challenges that were frightening. How does he do it? You know the drill. By the end of this chapter, you'll know the rest of the story.

THE LEGACY OF NORMAN COUSINS

The human body is its own best apothecary . . . because the most successful prescriptions are those filled by the body itself.

—Norman Cousins (1979)

We've all heard the saying, *those who laugh . . . last.* The incredible effects laughing has on the human body, as well as on our emotions, moods, and attitudes, have been documented and confirmed by anecdotal findings in medicine over the years. However, it was not until Norman Cousins, former editor of *Saturday Review,* wrote his pioneering self-discovery book, *Anatomy of An Illness as Perceived by the Patient* (1979), that the scientific world began to take the power of humor seriously.

Suffering from a debilitating and serious disease (ankylosing spondylitis, a degeneration of the spinal connective tissue), with no known cure, Cousins was given a 1 in 500 chance of recovery. Obviously frightened and concerned about this prognosis, he decided that he would involve himself in his survival, not his death.

Having read *The Wisdom of the Body* by Walter B. Cannon (1932) and Hans Seyle's classic book *The Stress of Life* (1976), Cousins recalled that these researchers had proven that negative emotions produced negative chemical changes in the body (as discussed in Chapter 1). Therefore, he reasoned that *positive* emotions would produce *positive* chemical changes. He wondered if emotions like love, hope, faith, and laughter could have a positive impact on his medical condition. Laughter was the first emotion Cousins chose to experiment with, and he decided to combine laughing with large doses of vitamin C.

He arranged with the hospital to bring a motion picture projector to his room, along with films of *Candid Camera,* the *Marx Brothers,* and the *Three Stooges* comedies. Remarkably, Cousins discovered that approximately 10 minutes of belly laughter had a significant anesthetic effect on him and resulted in at least two hours of pain-free sleep. Each time the pain returned, he turned on the projector again and laughed himself into a pain-free state.

So convinced was Cousins that it was his laughing that was impacting his bodily chemistry, that he had the nurses draw blood just before and several hours after the laughing episodes. Each time, his blood showed that his inflammation dropped. Not only was Cousins able to control pain through laughter, but also, astonishingly, his disease ultimately went into remission, never to reoccur!

Watch comedies on TV, and go to lighthearted, fun movies. Avoid the-sky-is-falling world news reports on TV and in the papers. Be selective in what you decide to watch on TV or at the theater. Ask yourself beforehand, "Is this show positive, upbeat, and life affirming, or is it negative, downbeat, and sure to leave me feeling worse?"

THE LEGACY OF MY DAD, BILL SINGER

My father was undoubtedly the funniest person I have ever known or seen on stage, screen, or TV. His sense of timing and extemporaneous ad-libbing kept the Singer family and their friends in hysterics for as long as I can remember.

Dad's sense of humor and remarkable memory for hundreds of jokes, suitable for any audience or occasion, served him well in his career as a traveling salesman. Although he was not an assertive person, Dad never had to twist arms to fill an order. He simply capitalized on the fact that buyers couldn't wait for Bill Singer to come to town with his spirit of playfulness and a new collection of jokes. Although the company he represented rarely offered the lowest or even the most competitive prices, orders were cheerfully written after the buyers spent hours laughing and having fun with Dad.

Shortly after his 79th birthday, Dad was rushed to a hospital in Florida with a grim series of diagnoses: He suffered heart failure, kidney failure, fluid in his lungs, and he was septic. He was put in the intensive care unit (ICU), put on a ventilator, and given a very poor prognosis.

My wife, Ronnie, and I were summoned by my uncle to come to Florida as quickly as possible. The tone of my uncle's voice was ominous—my father did not have long to live, and I should consider funeral arrangements.

When my wife and I arrived at the ICU, our hearts sank as we glanced through the window into Dad's room. There he was lying motionless with tubes everywhere, multiple IV lines, and a ventilator doing his breathing for him. My mother and uncle were standing next to him, looking grim, and feeling helpless. As a practicing clinical psychologist for many years, I have helped hundreds of people deal with the inevitable death of their loved ones. In fact, some of my most rewarding moments involve bringing a sense of peace to dying people, helping prepare them for their transition to the next place. Moreover, as a professional speaker, I have always been proud of my ability to motivate people so they can overcome any obstacles in their lives and find inspiration and happiness, despite their tragedies. But, that day, looking at my parents through that window, my mind was blank and my emotions overwhelming. Nothing I rehearsed on the airplane sounded appropriate, and overwhelming feelings of fear and sadness surrounded me.

Ronnie squeezed my hand, and we entered the room. My father was sleeping. We embraced my mother and my uncle. Suddenly, Dad opened his eyes, and seeing us, there was a bit of a smile, but even that was a struggle for him, and his color was ashen grey—an ominous sign. He couldn't talk because of the ventilator, so he motioned with his free hand that he could communicate to us by writing. Near the bed, we found a clipboard, a pencil, and some paper. Dad began to write very slowly. "I can't speak because of this darn tube in my throat, and it's so uncomfortable." We read the note and nodded sympathetically, squeezing Dad's hand.

Someone from social services then entered the room and told Dad that she had a delicate question to ask him. All ears were on her as she asked, "Mr. Singer, I know this is difficult, but would you be interested in donating any organs?"

Suddenly, a big twinkle appeared in Dad's eyes as he again reached for the clipboard. I knew that look. It was the look my dad always had when he invented a hilarious one-liner to perfectly fit a situation. He smiled as he wrote a response to the question, "Well, I once gave away a piano. Does that count?"

The room erupted in laughter when she read his response aloud. And that was the beginning of a flood of hilarious comments that Dad penned for his nurses, his doctors, his visitors, and us over the next three days. This playful banter went on for only three days. . . . You see, after the second day, when my Dad started laughing and writing hilarious anecdotes, his heart and kidneys began to function normally, the fluid cleared out of his lungs, he was no longer septic, and the ventilator was removed. His specialists couldn't explain how or why he suddenly reversed his medical symptoms.

His throat was raw, so he continued to write on the third day. Amazingly, dad was released from the hospital on the fourth day! Astonishingly, Dad spent only four days traveling from death's doorstep to recuperation. My father, at the ripe age of 79, actually *laughed himself back to health*. There is truth to the adage, *those who laugh last.*

Rx41
Stress
Mastery

Seek out every opportunity to belly laugh yourself to health.

WHAT DO YOU REALLY GET OUT OF LAUGHING?

A person without a sense of humor is like a wagon without springs—jostled by every pebble in the road.

—Henry Ward Beecher, clergyman,
abolitionist, and speaker

Drs. William Fry Jr. and Waleed Salameh (1986) have spent their careers studying and reporting on the impact of laughter on the body. Among their discoveries is the fact that most physiological systems in the body are directly affected by laughter. The cardiovascular system is exercised whenever you laugh, as your heart rate and blood pressure rise and fall. The heavy breathing connected with belly laughing is a healthy workout for your respiratory system. Muscles release tension as they tighten up and release. Perhaps most important, natural opiates, such as endorphins (a major immune system booster), are released into your bloodstream, creating feelings similar to the long-distance jogger's *runner's high*. It's well established, for example, that it is virtually impossible to be laughing heartily and be simultaneously angry. Creativity, energy, and motivation are all positively impacted by hearty laughter.

Some of the major research findings of the impact of laughter on the immune system comes from Dr. Lee Berk and Dr. Stanley Tan of Loma Linda University (HolisticOnline.com, n.d.).

To date their published studies have shown that laughing lowers blood pressure, reduces stress hormones, increases muscle flexion, and boosts immune function by raising levels of infection-fighting T-cells, disease-fighting proteins called Gamma-interferon and B-cells, which produce disease-destroying antibodies. Laughter also triggers the release of endorphins, the body's natural painkillers, and produces a general sense of well-being. (p. 1)

Not only does laughing stimulate the immune system, but even *anticipating* having a good laugh stimulates it and produces health-promoting hormones. Researchers at Loma Linda University recently discovered that people who *anticipate* that they will soon be laughing (for example, planning to go to a funny movie or selecting one on TV), increase their endorphin production and even increase the release of human growth hormone (a major antiaging hormone) by a whopping 87% (The American Physiological Society, 2008)!

It's clear that allowing yourself to laugh frequently is not only an excellent way to lower your stress level, but also it's a powerful stress and disease preventive. Incorporating laughter and fun into your daily activities is one of the best forms of preventive medicine you can give yourself.

TODAY'S UPSETS ARE TOMORROW'S LAUGHS

The crisis of today is the joke of tomorrow.

—H. G. Wells, author

We've all been there. You do or say something that is so embarrassing that you think you'll never survive it. Many teachers can cite the exact moment when they walked into their classroom trailing toilet paper behind them, with a portion of their skirt and the toilet paper neatly tucked into their underwear.

I vividly recall an incident that took place the evening before the most important presentation of my new career as a psychologist. I was invited to present the research results of my doctoral dissertation to the bigwigs at the Internal Revenue Service (IRS), who sponsored my project, which was a study of stress among IRS collection agents.

Unfortunately, the zipper on my pants burst the evening before my presentation and those were the only pants I brought with me. There were no tailor shops or men's clothing stores open that late, so I had to come up with a creative solution.

Although I was mortified, I said those fateful words to myself, "Jack, someday this will make a great story. You'll be laughing about this. Just use creative thinking and you'll come up with a solution." I suppose that if this incident took place today, I would add the phrase, "It is what it is, Jack. Deal with it."

The next morning, I borrowed some large safety pins and pinned my fly shut. Because the pants fit so tightly, the fly was still pulling open, so I made my tie very long and pinned it to my fly, forcing me to walk bent over. I then buttoned my jacket closed and was pleased with my novel solution to this embarrassing problem.

I arrived at the IRS building promptly at 7:15 a.m. It was a hot and muggy August day in Washington. A security guard saw me hobble out of the cab, so he took my arm to help me up the front stairs. The guard was fanning himself with his clipboard on this very hot morning. I told him that I was there to see the director and his staff, and the guard informed me that the air conditioner was broken in the building and all of the directors were casual, having removed their jackets and ties. "They'll tell you to remove your jacket and tie and get as comfortable as possible!"

At that moment, all I could visualize was appearing before this esteemed audience and looking like an idiot, declining to remove my jacket in the sweltering heat.

I entered the boardroom and all of the IRS big shots were there, in shirtsleeves, of course. It felt like 110 degrees in that room. They insisted that I remove my jacket and tie and make myself comfortable.

"No way," I blurted out. Composing myself, I continued, "I actually feel a bit chilly," as perspiration was pouring down my forehead and soaking my shirt.

Finally, I got into my presentation, and I could actually feel myself getting more comfortable as I got into my presentation because the pins were holding. I told myself that I was going to be able to pull this off under such difficult circumstances. As I was reaching the end, I thought to myself, "Only a few minutes to go; I'll take a couple of questions, tell them I have a flight to catch, make my exit, and be on my way home with my secret undetected."

I completed the talk and opened the floor for questions. A gentleman, sitting far in the back of the room, immediately raised his hand. My knee-jerk reaction was to acknowledge the questioner by pointing to him, momentarily forgetting my predicament. So as I raised my hand and stretched it out in his direction, I screamed, "Yessss, dddooo yyyyou hhhave a quessssstion?" You see, the instant that I stretched my arm out and pointed to him, I felt a pain I cannot describe. I realized that one of the safety pins popped open and was stabbing me!

Life is so unpredictable. We never know when uncomfortable, embarrassing, or humiliating circumstances will befall us. Little did I know then that someday I would use my IRS adventure as a signature story in the speeches and workshops I conduct, showing people the magnificent benefits of laughter, fun, and humor and how not to stress over circumstances beyond their control. And little did I realize at the time that I would use this story to make a point in a stress-mastery guide for teachers.

It's been said that *humor equals tragedy plus time*. Regardless of the circumstances, you can always buffer yourself with the thought that "Someday, I'll be laughing about this!"

Whatever seems unbearable or embarrassing today will be hilarious down the road. Tell yourself, "Someday, I'll be laughing about this."

LIGHTEN UP YOUR CLASSROOM

At a public function, Lady Astor once commented to an inebriated and rude Winston Churchill, "Sir, if I was your wife, I would surely put poison in your tea." Churchill quickly retorted, "Madam, if you were my wife, I would surely drink it!"

When I reflect on my elementary, junior high, and

Good News!

You don't have to be a great joke teller to bring wonderful, healthy humor into your life.

high school educations, the teachers who immediately jump into my memory are those who brought fun and laughter into the classroom. I remember my geometry teacher in high school pretending that he was senile and wondering aloud if he was in the right room, as the entire class quietly hid in the cloakroom just before the bell rang to begin class. I remember my sixth-grade teacher having talent shows on Friday afternoons so we could practice expressing our hidden talents in front of our classmates. I always looked forward to those Friday afternoons!

Bringing fun to any learning situation promotes both attention and retention of the material. Johnny Carson once observed, "People will pay much more to be entertained than to be educated." Professional speakers understand this concept, and the best ones fill their presentations with humor. Opening the presentation with humor builds a positive, relaxed climate and gives the audience an expectation of safety. It relaxes the audience and makes them more receptive to learning the messages that the speaker is imparting. Every book on public speaking discusses the tremendous impact of sprinkling humor throughout a speech.

This concept holds true for any learning situation, particularly the classroom. Researchers studying humor in the classroom found that students in classrooms of teachers who used humor frequently retained more information than those in classes where teachers did not use humor very often. Moreover, surveys of students in college found that they believed they learned more in their precollege years from teachers who frequently used humor in class (Kher, Molstad, & Donahue, 1999).

Using jokes to explain concepts enhances listening skills and creativity. Test scores rise as students recall concepts from memory because the learning was tied to a joke or something humorous (Flowers, 2001). As the students have more fun and learn more, their stress levels are reduced (Garner, 2006), and *your* stress level will be reduced at the same time; you prevent stress because the teaching environment in that classroom is so much more relaxed and the students are so much more motivated.

John Morreall, in his book, *Humor Works* (1997), described a second-grade teacher who came to his humor seminar and shared a fascinating experience she had when she gave a writing assignment in which she asked her students to describe the kind of person they wanted to marry. One young girl wrote, "I want to marry someone who can make me laugh without tickling me."

It has been reported that the average child laughs about 150 times a day, while the average adult laughs only about 15 times a day (Miglino, 2009). Sadly, as we grow older, we are told that laughing, giggling, and having fun are behaviors reserved for children. We often bury the child within us, believing that laughing is a sign of insincerity or immaturity.

When students are having fun, while feeling safe and supported by one another and the teacher, they are in position to break through self-imposed barriers and limitations, and their learning and retention both skyrocket. Here is an example of a joke a teacher used with her high school students:

A driver was pulled over by a female police officer for speeding. As the officer was writing the ticket, she noticed several machetes in the car. "What are those for?" she asked suspiciously. "I'm a juggler," the man replied. "I use those in my act." "Well prove that and show me," the officer demanded. So he got out the machetes and started juggling them, first three, then more, and finally seven at one time, overhand, underhand, behind the back, putting on a dazzling show and amazing the officer. Another car passed by, and the driver did a double take and said, "Oh my gosh! I will never drink and drive. Look at the sobriety test they're giving now!"

So how can you simultaneously enable your students to laugh and learn? There is no limit to the creative ideas you can come up with to keep them smiling and learning.

Find creative ways to bring fun and humor to your classroom.

In this chapter, there are many examples of successful methods that teachers have reported for bringing fun to their classrooms. Obviously, your use of various techniques depends on the age appropriateness of them, and this list only scratches the surface. You'll find many more examples in the references at the end of the chapter, and by simply Googling "classroom humor," you will find many jokes, anecdotes, and cartoons you can use with your students.

Allow me to give you a word of caution here. Providing a fun atmosphere in the classroom can be very rewarding, but it should never be at the expense of the teacher. Allowing students to disrupt the teacher's lesson with spontaneous blurting out of funny comments should not be accepted or classroom management surely will be compromised. Young teachers may be tempted to allow this kind of banter because of their need to be liked by their students, but the long-term effects of this may certainly backfire because an atmosphere of disrespect may become acceptable. So, as you review the next examples, keep in mind that you never want to compromise your curriculum or your classroom management.

Make Your Classroom a Place to Have Fun While Learning

Enforce the rules to keep the class professional and on task, but give leeway for spirited excitement with projects, and even encourage class clowns to use the class as a forum for shredding their own inhibitions and testing their ability to get a spontaneous laugh, as long as their humor is never at anyone's expense or inappropriate. Theme days are also a great way to generate fun in a learning environment.

Consider Starting Each Day With the Joke of the Day

Scan the Internet or joke books for examples. Have a contest each week for the funniest joke or cartoon that students bring to class; post them and give goofy prizes, such as clown noses, to the winner.

Intersperse Your Curriculum With
Fun Activities That Encourage Group Identity

Cultivating and nurturing fun and humor in the classroom this way will generate camaraderie. Use a funny top-10 list to help students memorize facts. This is also very useful on the first day of class, when you could open with, "Here are the top-10 things you should know about your teacher." Then, have students introduce themselves the same way. First impressions last, so if your first day in class is fun, you will have your students excited about your class, even on days when you don't have the time to have fun. They'll think more fun is on its way any day now.

Allow the Students to Generate
Laughs While They Work on Projects

Set the rule that humor in bad taste or humor at the expense of another student will not be tolerated, but allow the creative use of humor and fun as adjuncts to the learning objectives.

Fill Your Classroom With Joke Books

Garfield and *The Far Side* are two excellent examples of cartoon books you can have available. Pin up funny quotes from famous people. As an example, playwright George Bernard Shaw once wrote to Winston Churchill. "Dear Mr. Churchill: Enclosed are two tickets to my new play, which opens Thursday night. Please come and bring a friend, if you have one."

Sir Winston replied, "I am sorry; I have a previous engagement and cannot attend your opening. However, I will come to the second performance, if there is one."

Have Dress-Up Days

Many lessons in history, for example, can be injected with fun by having the teacher and students dress up in homemade era costumes. For instance, if you're teaching art, put some bandages on your left ear and have some paintbrushes sticking out of your pocket, and poof—you're a perfect Vincent van Gogh. For music, find an old beat-up trumpet and bend the bell to describe the wonders of Dizzy Gillespie.

Use Improvisation Games to Anchor Learning Points

The clever use of improvisational (improv) games to anchor learning points is something you can use immediately. In the references at the end of this chapter, I have included an easy-to-implement book on improv games for children (Bedore, 2004).

One of the greatest benefits of improv games in school is that it forces camaraderie and builds teams. Children are hardwired for imagination and adventure, so to make up stuff is easy. Other benefits of improv games are learning to adapt to unforeseen changes, developing self-confidence, practicing creative thinking, strengthening speaking and listening skills, learning the concept of cooperation, building frustration tolerance and acceptance of others, and enhancing social skills. Need I say more? What a powerful teaching tool, and the games can be learning points from your curriculum.

An improv game called A&E Biography is inspired by the cable channel A&E and its *Biography* series. The teacher asks the students to select a historical character whom they are studying. One player, the host, introduces the character and discusses highlights of his or her life. Then, the host discusses key situations in that person's life and chooses players to portray those situations in a fun way. For example, as the host begins, "Life for Lincoln was very harsh in the early years . . ." the teacher stops and selects another student to act out this harsh beginning. All students get a chance to act out parts of Lincoln's life.

LIGHTEN UP BOTH YOUR SCHOOL AND YOUR LIFE

Happiness is like perfume . . . when you sprinkle it on others, you can't help but get a few drops on yourself.

—Ralph Waldo Emerson, essayist and poet

The staff that has fun together will bond as a team, without backstabbing, vying for power with one another, and so on. Besides bringing fun and humor into the classroom, you can bring it to your school (see Weinstein & Goodman, 1980) and, of course, your home life.

First and Foremost, Make a Humor Commitment to Yourself

Write down on paper or on your computer the following letter:

Dear _____

(your name)

I promise to bring more laughter to both my school and home life and to make note of every humorous opportunity that comes my way.

Jokingly,

_____

(your signature)

P.S. Once I accomplish the above, I will reward myself with _____.

In Your School, Have a Positive Party Funded by Negative People

Make a rule that any administrator, teacher, or staff person caught making negative comments to or about *anyone* (student, parent, colleague, someone on the phone—anyone) throws 50 cents into a kitty kept in the office and humorously labeled as the "Positive Party Kitty." At the end of a month or two, use that money to fund a positive party for everyone, and be sure to "recognize" the key contributors.

Sneak a Humorous Item Onto the Agenda of Every Serious Meeting

For example, slip onto the serious agenda, "The tattoo and body piercing clinic will be held right after the meeting." This will catch everyone by surprise when they read it and should lighten things up.

Provide Popsicles for the Teacher, Administrator, or Staff Person Who Puts Up With the Most Heat During the Day

It helps when your colleagues recognize what you are going through, and this can be accompanied by a brainstorming session, where everyone can discuss the best way to handle a situation like the one you bring up. Keep an ample supply of popsicles in a refrigerator in or near the front office.

Start Bad Days With an Improvised Song

When it's a tough day and you or your colleagues are having difficulties, sing to one another for a minute or two about the work challenges. Sing to the tune of familiar songs. Perhaps give a prize to the best composition of the day. Try it. Before you know it, you'll all be laughing together!

Start a New, Fun Practice at the School: When People Are Having a Bad Day, They Can Ask for a Standing Ovation

Walk into the teacher's lounge and shout, "I just finished dealing with the most obnoxious parents you can imagine, and I need a standing ovation!" You can bring this into the classroom and encourage your students to ask for a standing ovation after completing projects or even their homework. "I just finished my biology project, and I want a standing ovation!" Encourage thunderous explosions of cheering, table pounding, and whistling from the other students.

Have Your Own Personal Stress-Survival Kit

This can be kept at home and be made up of joke books, funny videos, and the like that you can pull out after especially difficult days. Blow bubbles. Use paddleball toys. Don't be afraid to let the little kid in you come out frequently.

Make Goofy Faces Every Time You Are in Front of a Mirror

It's important to get rid of that stern teacher's expression, and allow yourself to be silly sometimes. Looking at the variety of faces you have in your repertoire will help you choose which you will use that day as you relate something funny to your class. It's also a good idea to lead an enthusiastic cheer for yourself in the mirror before you leave for school. "I am awesome, and I will laugh away my stress today." The mirror is also a wonderful place to practice smiling, especially if you do not naturally smile. Force yourself to smile and see how much better you feel than when you portray that natural frown and furled eyebrows. If you have trouble smiling, get one of those cardboard smiley faces on a stick, hold it in front of your face, and look in the mirror. That should do it. When you smile more, even if put on, you start to feel better, and those around you catch it. It's contagious!

At Least Once a Week, Make Contact With a Friend Who Makes You Laugh

So many teachers surround themselves with bitter, negative, and moody colleagues. You need to have at least one friend who is cheerful, funny, and positive, and be sure to speak to that person as much as you can.

So now, you know what a powerful stress preventer and reducer it is to laugh often and to put fun into your teaching, your interactions with colleagues, and your whole life. Besides the stress benefits, your whole body will benefit. As well-known professional speaker Michael Pritchard says, "You don't stop laughing because you grow old; you grow old because you stop laughing!"

Avoid negative people, and if you cannot avoid them altogether, let their negative messages and feedback about you go in one ear and out the other. Notice the good things you love about the people in your life, and ignore the things you don't love about them. Make sure there are happy, fun-loving people in your life, and stay away from bitter, disgruntled people.

Oh, yes, back to our music teacher and band director, Rich M. How has he maintained such a terrific record of never having a student talk back to him or ever having to send a student to the principal, with all sorts of students throughout more than 42 years of teaching? In his words,

> *It is not uncommon for me to go to jokes on the Internet before going to bed. Many times, I print really good ones and spring them on the kids the following day. Sometimes, I'll start my class with one, but that doesn't work for a lot of people because they can't quiet the kids down after the laughter. I always have something to go into right away.*
>
> *Many times, in the middle of nowhere, I'll pause and say, "Hey did you hear the one about . . ." At the end of the year, when my students write in my yearbook, most of the time they comment on my sense of humor and how I made them laugh! It's very rewarding.*
>
> *Kate, a sixth grader, wrote, "Mr. M., you have a great sense of humor and you make band so much fun! This school is so lucky to have you!"*
>
> *Briton, a sixth grader, wrote, "Thank you so much for being there for me on my bad days so you could cheer me up!"*
>
> *Andrea, an eighth grader wrote, "I don't know what I would've done in junior high without you. Every year we get new teachers but, by being in band, I always had you and looked forward to your class! I will miss your jokes and all the great times we had this year. I'm grateful to have met you!" (personal communication)*

Remember, you don't have to be a great joke teller to keep your students laughing and motivated; just scan the Internet and joke books and consider assigning students to bring in jokes and cartoons.

ACTION PLAN FOR STRESS MASTERY

Table 7.1	My Action Plan for Stress Mastery

Check off when completed.	
New Behavior	*What I Did and the Date Accomplished*
❏ I will look for examples of humor all around me and make note of them. ❏ ❏ ❏	What I did: Date accomplished:
❏ I will look for opportunities to belly laugh each day and make note of them. ❏ ❏ ❏	What I did: Date accomplished:
❏ When I am in an embarrassing situation, I will visualize laughing about it in the future. ❏ ❏ ❏	What I did: Date accomplished:
❏ I will blend fun into my teaching to lighten up my classroom. ❏ ❏ ❏	What I did: Date accomplished:
❏ I will suggest ways to lighten up my school's staff and administration. ❏ ❏ ❏	What I did: Date accomplished:

(Continued)

Table 7.1	(Continued)	
☐ I will make adding fun to my life and my family a priority. ☐ ☐ ☐	What I did: Date accomplished:

REFERENCES

American Physiological Society. (2008, April). *More on the humor health connection: New study finds anticipating a laugh reduces stress hormones.* Retrieved May 19, 2009, from http://www.the-aps.org/press/journal/08/14.htm.

Bedore, R. (2004). *101 improv games for children and adults.* Berkeley, CA: Hunter House.

Cannon, W. B. (1932). *The wisdom of the body.* New York: Norton.

Cousins, N. (1979). *Anatomy of an illness as perceived by the patient.* New York: Norton.

Flowers, J. (2001, May/June). The value of humor in technology education. *The Technology Teacher, 60*(8), 10–13.

Fry, W. F., & Salameh, W. A. (Eds.). (1986). *Handbook of humor and psychotherapy.* Sarasota, FL: Professional Resource Exchange.

Garner, R. L. (2006). Humor in pedagogy: How ha-ha can lead to aha! *College Teaching, 54*(1), 177–180.

Greenwich, C. (1998). *The fun factor.* New York: McGraw-Hill.

HolisticOnline.com. (n.d.). *Therapeutic benefits of laughter.* Retrieved June 16, 2009, from http://www.holisticonline.com/Humor_Therapy/humor_Therapy_benefits.htm.

Kher, N., Molstad, S., & Donahue, R. (1999). Using humor in the college classroom to enhance teaching effectiveness in "dread courses." *College Student Journal, 33,* 400.

Miglino, M. (2009, March 25). *Laugh riot.* Retrieved June 14, 2009, from http://www.timesunion.com/Aspstories/story.asp?storyID=7804098category=LifeAtHome& BCCode=&newsdate=5/23/2009.

Morreall, J. (1997). *Humor works.* Amherst, MA: HRD Press.

Russell, J. (2007, December). *Using humor in the classroom.* Retrieved April 12, 2009, from http://els.earlham.Edu/spe/files/30/226/JimR_2008.pdf.

Seyle, H. (1976). *The stress of life.* New York: Ballantine Books.

Weinstein, M., & Goodman, J. (1980). *Playfair.* San Luis Obispo, CA: Impact.

8

How to Become and Remain a Resilient Person

A pessimist is one who makes difficulties of his opportunities; an optimist is one who makes opportunities of his difficulties.

—Reginald B. Mansell, author

LEARNING OBJECTIVES

- I will understand the specific characteristics of optimistic and pessimistic interpretations of events in my life.
- I will understand the relationship between events in my life, my interpretation of those events, and, ultimately, my vulnerability to disease.
- I will be able to use the A-B-C-D-E model for developing optimistic thinking.
- I will be able to use the Thinking-Pattern Worksheet (TPW) to convert pessimistic thinking to optimistic thinking.
- I will learn many additional stress buffers that I will incorporate into my ongoing efforts to build resilience.

ongratulations! You are almost finished learning how to master the stresses in your life. Certainly, by now, you must be very optimistic that you can turn the corner, take charge of your life, and begin to feel consistently better. In case there is still a glimmer of self-doubt remaining, let's learn about how to boost your optimism, or if you are a pessimist, learn how to turn that kind of negative thinking around quickly. A large part of remaining resilient in the face of stressful situations is having an *optimistic* attitude.

Mike L. is a high school science teacher. Over the years, he consistently found himself buried under 14-hour workdays, having difficulty finding enough time to devote to his family, and strained each day to get motivated enough to inspire his students. But despite these challenges, throughout his career, Mike has remained resilient and optimistic. In fact, this year he was recognized by *USA Today* as an All-USA Teacher. How does he do it? When you discover his creative ideas at the end of this chapter, you'll find many that you can incorporate into your work and life immediately.

LEARNING TO BECOME OPTIMISTIC

Quit now, you'll never make it. If you disregard this advice, you'll be halfway there.

—David Zucker, film director

Let's begin with some definitions. Looking at the glass as half empty or half full doesn't give you the whole story of optimism versus pessimism, although there is some validity to that commonly used definition. Optimism and pessimism are really about how you interpret or explain bad and good events that take place in your life and your expectations about whether those kinds of events will continue to occur (Seligman, 1998).

As you can see summarized in Table 8.1, optimists explain that bad things take place in their lives because of external factors, representing *isolated* and temporary setbacks, unlikely to be repeated and not their fault. Circumstances beyond their control, bad luck, and the behaviors of other people all may contribute to this misfortune. They might say something like, "This was awful, but I couldn't do anything about it; it was a fluke, probably will never happen again, and it will not affect any other part of my life."

Because they believe that better days will soon be here, they see misfortune and defeat as temporary setbacks and as signals to dig in and try harder. This way of interpreting difficult events motivates them to persevere and take charge of their lives to maximize the chances that better days will soon be here.

Table 8.1   Characteristics of Optimistic and Pessimistic Interpretations

When Bad Things Happen	
Optimistic Orientation	**Pessimistic Orientation**
• *"This was a fluke. It's not my fault. I had a bad day at school because I didn't get enough sleep last night."* (external cause) • *"I can control these things and make sure they don't happen again. I wasn't as prepared as I should have been before meeting my administrator and that's why she didn't grant my request. I will make sure that doesn't happen next time."* (control) • *"This kind of event is unlikely to repeat itself. I lost my temper with that parent only because he was in a bad mood when he came into my room, and he was rude to me."* (specific and temporary)	• "Bad things happen because of my lack of skills; it's my fault. I will continue to have bad days at school no matter what I do because I'm not cut out for this occupation." (internal cause) • "Bad things will continue to happen to me, no matter what I do." (learned helplessness) • "I didn't make a good impression in my meeting with the administrator because I always screw up these kinds of meetings." • "Bad things always happen to me and will continue to happen in many areas of my life." (hopelessness) • "I lost my temper with that parent because I am impatient and will never be able to assert myself calmly with rude parents." (permanent and pervasive)
When Good Things Happen	
Optimistic Interpretation	**Pessimistic Interpretation**
• *"Good things came about because of my skills, effort, and/or motivation. I was voted Teacher of the Year because of all of the effort I put into my teaching skills."* (control) • *"Good things will continue to occur over time. No matter how many disruptive kids I have in my classroom, I will always be able to manage my classroom with creative solutions."* (permanent) • *"Good things will happen across many aspects of my life."* (pervasive) • *"Because I'm smart and creative, good things will happen in many aspects of my life."*	• "This was a fluke. I was just lucky. I was lucky to win the Teacher of the Year award. They just didn't have anyone else who could qualify this year." (lack of control) • "This is not likely to happen again. I was just lucky to get good teacher ratings this year because I didn't have too many kids in class who were disruptive." (temporary) • "Good things generally will not happen to me." (specific occurrence) • "Maybe I do well teaching, but my family life and my social life are a mess."

Critics say that such thinking avoids taking responsibility for failure by simply finding excuses and blaming others. Whether this argument has any credence is irrelevant because such optimistic thinking most often leads to successful outcomes in the future. For decades, researchers have reported these positive outcomes in a diverse array of situations, including helping athletes win after losses, building one's immune system, warding off diseases, and even helping breast cancer victims live longer (Haven, Frandsen, Karren, & Hooker, 1992; Peterson & Bossio, 1993; Seligman, 1998; Siegel, 1998; Sobel & Ornstein, 1996).

On the other hand, when good things happen to optimists, they use the opposite thinking to explain those events. They believe those good outcomes happened precisely because of their own motivation and hard work and that such good outcomes will repeat themselves many times. After good things happen, they might say to themselves, "This is the way my life goes. Good things always happen to me in all sorts of situations, and it's because of my efforts that they happen that way." Optimists take credit for good outcomes and blame bad outcomes on external factors.

Pessimists, on the other hand, explain unfortunate events that occur in their lives as *chronic* and *permanent* setbacks caused by their inadequacies, and therefore, they expect bad things to happen to them repeatedly. In short, it was their fault that these events turned out the way they did. Consequently, pessimists often feel helpless, hopeless, and trapped in life circumstances that they believe are unlikely to change.

Martin Seligman (1998), who is the father of this pioneering research, calls this *learned helplessness*. Pessimists believe that they have no control over what happens to them in life, and therefore, whatever they do won't matter.

When good things happen to pessimists, they attribute those outcomes to luck and take no credit for them. "It doesn't matter what I do; I will never be successful. On the few occasions when I was successful, I was just lucky."

Not surprisingly, there is much scientific research showing that people who maintain an optimistic orientation toward life are healthier, suffer fewer catastrophic illnesses, and actually live longer than do pessimists. Seligman (1998), who insists that optimistic thinking can be learned at any age, reports studies in which having an optimistic orientation at age 45 is the primary determinant of the health of these people over the next twenty years.

Figure 8.1	The Relationship Between Events, Pessimistic Interpretations, and Disease Vulnerability

(1) →	(2) →	(3) →	(4) →	(5) →	(6)
Activating event	Pessimistic interpretation	Depression, hopelessness	Transmitter hormone depletion	Immune system suppression	Vulnerability to disease

Here's how Seligman (1998) and others (Sapolsky, 1998) explain what happens. As you can see in Figure 8.1, life events and experiences that are interpreted in pessimistic ways lead to the emotional consequences of hopelessness, helplessness, and depression (i.e., stress outcomes). In an effort to fight the source of the stress, there is a resultant depletion in the nerve-transmission-receptor hormones. Your brain doesn't know whether your stress is from surgery, childbirth, an auto accident in which you were injured, or from hopeless feelings. Therefore, the pessimism, helplessness and hopelessness that you feel from specific events in your life, and the negative, pessimistic way in which you interpret them, results in the same depletion of neurotransmitters that would occur if you were injured or dealing with an emergency situation. Recall that the SNS (sympathetic nervous system) switches on whenever you are stressed and have negative, self-defeating thoughts and beliefs, such as hopeless and helpless feelings.

When the brain recognizes this depletion, it then suppresses the immune system because in a real emergency it's not efficient to be working on long-term immunity strengthening; instead, the body works on dealing with the urgent situation. While the immune system is shutting down, the production of disease-killing T cells shuts down, as well as the production of natural-killer cells, whose purpose is to recognize bacteria, disease invaders, and foreign cells that attempt to invade the body. You can imagine the vulnerability to disease that this series of events leads to.

In summary, when one views events in a pessimistic, helpless, and hopeless way, the emergency system is continuously turned on, thus shutting down the immune system and leading to increased susceptibility to disease. So it's certainly not surprising that countless studies conclude that people who have a consistently pessimistic orientation suffer from far more illnesses than do optimists, and optimists outlive pessimists (Seligman, 1998).

The positive health outcomes for optimistically oriented people are replicated with a whole host of studies also reported by Seligman (1998). Although no claim is made that optimism can overcome a terminal (lethal) amount of cancer (although famed author and physician Bernie Siegel [1986, 1998] would argue that such miracles are possible using positive affirmations), Seligman (1998) concludes, from the scientific evidence, that "Psychological traits, particularly optimism, can produce good health. This evidence makes sense of—and supersedes—the torrent of personal stories in which states ranging from laughter to the will to live appear to help health" (p. 173). In fact, he cites research that shows that even when people have an unrealistically optimistic view of their future—such as denying the severity of an illness—this belief structure, alone, may significantly help them cope and can extend their lives.

We now know that your personality is not necessarily set in stone. Regardless of your hardwiring, you can learn new, more healthy behaviors, and with practice (the magic 21 days), optimistic thinking habits can take the place of pessimistic thinking habits. Furthermore, you now know that if you have had many stress-causing events take place in the last 12 months, you can control new events from affecting you in the coming months, by delaying them.

Seligman's books (1998, 2002) are filled with methods for building an optimistic explanatory style, both for adults and children. The results of his research show that both adults and children reduce their risk of depression, boost their self-esteem, and enhance their physical health by practicing the skills he teaches.

Good News!

You have already learned the key elements of changing your thinking from pessimistic to optimistic thinking! Review the TPW from Chapter 5.

| Figure 8.2 | The A-B-C-D-E Model for Developing Optimistic Thinking |

(A) →	(B) →	(C) →	(D) →	(E)
Activating event (stress causing)	Negative beliefs about A	Consequent emotions (pessimistic, hopeless, helpless)	Disputing thoughts	Energized emotions (optimistic, hopeful, in control)

The main premise of these books is learning to use the **A-B-C-D-E** method of examining provocative events and the resultant negative thoughts. As you saw in Chapter 5, the most important skill to be developed is to find logical rebuttal thoughts that dispute the original pessimistic thoughts. Once you do this, the original negative emotions give way to healthy, energized emotions. (See Figure 8.2.)

Rx45
Stress Mastery

Using the TPWs in Tables 8.2 and 8.3, practice interpreting unfortunate events in your mind in optimistic ways.

The TPW is again the vehicle by which we can learn to identify our distorted-thinking patterns that lead to pessimistic, helpless feelings and dispute them on the spot. This sample TPW shows the beliefs (thoughts) and the disputed thinking of a pessimistic teacher.

It's important to be very adamant about disputing those thoughts. Use your rubber band and shout, "Stop!" to yourself once you recognize that you are engaging in negative, pessimistic thoughts. In the Table 8.2

Table 8.2   Sample Thinking-Pattern Worksheet (TPW) for Optimism

Description of the situation that led to *pessimistic*, emotional reactions:

"I came home from school today, completely drained. I don't like several of my students, and I don't have patience for their disruptive behavior." **(A)**

Negative emotions **(C)** prior to disputing my thoughts and their intensity (1–10):

1. "I'm feeling overwhelmed, and I don't see how this can ever get better." (10)
2. "I'm feeling frightened about my future as a teacher." (6)
3. "I feel hopeless and helpless." (8)

Automatic Thoughts and Beliefs (B)	Self-Defeating Thinking Pattern	Disputing Responses (Rebuttal) (D)
1. "My class is a disaster. I'm feeling overwhelmed, and I don't see how this can ever get better."	a. *Overgeneralization* b. *Magnification*	a. "There is no need to magnify or blow things out of proportion. I had hoped for a better classroom situation, but this is not the end of the world. Every teacher feels overwhelmed at times. This is mainly because of the large number of students I have, not because of my incompetence. I have resources to review that will show me ways to control my students, and I will have better days in the future."
2. "I don't think I will ever be happy teaching. I don't see how I will ever be happy in this job."	a. *Fortune-telling* b. *Emotional reasoning*	a. "Does this experience really mean that I will never be successful? I have dealt with adversity before in my life and not had to run away. I will talk to my colleagues about strategies to make my job more pleasant."
3. "This is really happening because I don't have what it takes to be a successful teacher."	a. *All or nothing* b. *Blaming* c. *Emotional reasoning*	a. "The principal hired me because he saw something in me that he predicted would make me successful, and success is not simply based on one or two days of experience."

(Continued)

Table 8.2   (Continued)

Negative emotions **after** rebutting my thoughts and their intensity (1–10):

1. "I'm feeling overwhelmed." (3)
2. "I'm feeling frightened." (1)
3. "I'm very worried." (2)
4. _____
5. _____

Self-Defeating Thinking Patterns: all or nothing; magnification; mind reading; catastrophizing; being right; should, have to, must; control fallacy; overgeneralization; blaming; and emotional reasoning

Adapted from Matthew McKay and Martha Davis. *Thoughts and Feelings.*, 1981, with permission from New Harbinger Press.

example, this teacher has the belief that her classroom situation "can never get better." This is a classic example of *magnification* and blowing the situation out of proportion in her mind. She must dispute such a thought vehemently, with a rational rebuttal, such as the following:

> *There is no need to magnify or blow things out of proportion. I had hoped for a better classroom situation, but this is not the end of the world. Every teacher feels overwhelmed at times. This is mainly because of the large number of students I have, not because of my incompetence. I have resources to review that will show me ways to control my students, and I will have better days in the future.*

Once you realize that it is your *distorted* beliefs and thoughts **(B)** about your classroom situation(s) **(A)** that are the cause of your pessimism and hopeless and helpless feelings **(C)** (rather than chronic weaknesses within yourself), you can vehemently dispute **(D)** those beliefs and thoughts, resulting in energized **(E)**, revitalized feelings and emotions and a more optimistic outlook.

When you are in the process of disputing the distorted beliefs, ask yourself the following: "What evidence is there that supports my belief? Are there any alternative explanations for my conclusions? Does holding on to this belief serve any useful purpose?"

A blank TPW is provided for you in Table 8.3. As before, make several copies of this form to use, and use it every time you feel down, stressed, helpless, overwhelmed, and, particularly, pessimistic. If you are conscientious about using a TPW every time you begin to feel negative emotions, you will quickly learn how to recognize and dispute your internal self-talk

Table 8.3   Blank Thinking-Pattern Worksheet (TPW) for Optimism

Make copies of this table before you fill it in so you can fill in the blank spaces every time you feel pessimistic emotions.

Description of the situation that led to *pessimistic*, emotional reactions:

1. —————————————————————————————
2. —————————————————————————————
3. —————————————————————————————

Negative emotions (C) prior to disputing my thoughts and their intensity (1–10):

1. —————————————————————————————
2. —————————————————————————————
3. —————————————————————————————

Automatic Thoughts and Beliefs (B)	*Self-Defeating Thinking Pattern*	Disputing Responses (Rebuttal) (D)
1.	*a.* *b.*	1.
2.	*a.* *b.*	2.
3.	*a.* *b.*	3.
4.	*a.* *b.*	4.

If you have more than four thoughts, continue this on another sheet.

Negative emotions after rebutting my thoughts and their intensity (1–10):

1. —————————————————————————————
2. —————————————————————————————
3. —————————————————————————————
4. —————————————————————————————
5. —————————————————————————————

Self-Defeating Thinking Patterns: all or nothing; magnification; mind reading; catastrophizing; being right; should, have to, must; control fallacy; overgeneralization; blaming; and emotional reasoning

Adapted from Matthew McKay and Martha Davis. *Thoughts and Feelings.*, 1981, with permission from New Harbinger Press.

distortions that have led to your unhappiness and pessimistic attitudes. About how many days will it take of consistently practicing this skill to make a permanent change in your pessimistic views of your life? Right—21 days.

Perhaps the best example of remaining optimistic in the face of defeat is represented by this gentleman's life. Here is a series of life events that befell him:

> He failed in business and suffered bankruptcy in 1831.
>
> He was defeated in a run for state legislature in 1832.
>
> He failed again in business and again suffered bankruptcy in 1834.
>
> His fiancé died in 1835.
>
> He suffered a nervous breakdown in 1836.
>
> He was again defeated in election in 1838.
>
> He was defeated running for U.S. Congress in 1843.
>
> He was defeated again running for U.S. Congress in 1846.
>
> Once again, he was defeated running for U.S. Congress in 1848.
>
> He was defeated running for U.S. Senate in 1855.
>
> He was defeated trying to become U.S. Vice President in 1856.
>
> He was again defeated running for U.S. Senate in 1858.

Who could possibly come away from this series of defeats and tragedies and remain optimistic that success was still around the corner? The answer is . . . (drum roll please) . . . **Abraham Lincoln**, elected President of the United States in 1860.

HOW TO BRING MORE JOY AND HAPPINESS INTO YOUR LIFE

Appreciating the beauty of a blossom, the loveliness of a lilac, or the grace of a gazelle are ways in which people can . . . fill their daily lives with . . . pleasure.

—David Buss, author and psychologist

As you have probably noticed, I am a huge fan of the groundbreaking work of Dr. Martin Seligman and his positive psychology approach to helping people find lasting joy and happiness in their lives. A more recent book of his, *Authentic Happiness: Using the New Positive Psychology to Realize Your Potential for Lasting Fulfillment* (2002), is packed with self-surveys and practical, well-researched ideas to enrich your life and fulfill your dreams. Armed with insight from the surveys, you can choose specific strategies that Seligman provides for skyrocketing your joy and happiness, permanently!

I strongly recommend reading Seligman's books, but here's a jump start of five Stress Mastery Prescriptions that his research results recommend. You can start working on these today:

Sustain deep relationships with family and friends, and if possible, maintain a love relationship with a spouse or partner.

Volunteer and give of yourself to ease the plight of others.

Practice random acts of kindness on a regular basis (e.g., let a harried mother get in front of you in line or bring Sunday dinner to an elderly couple).

Maintain close ties to your religion or spiritual foundation, with faith in a good future guiding you. Pray regularly.

Prescription 50 is one that I completed while I was in Denver giving a speech to teachers. As I was suggesting to my audience that they should pay a gratitude visit to a mentor or someone who has been a special person in their lives, it occurred to me that I had never done that for one of the most important people who ever crossed paths with me, a professor at Colorado State University, just up I-25 from Denver. I made the call, drove up, visited, and he and I both had one of the most emotionally fulfilling experiences of our lives.

Think of a person in your life who has meant a lot to you, but to whom you have never fully expressed your appreciation. It could be a teacher, mentor, relative, friend, or anyone. Take your time composing a letter of appreciation to that person with the details of events that made this person so special to you and have the letter laminated. Then, contact that person and arrange for an in-person visit. Don't tell him or her the purpose of the visit, and be sure to bring the laminated letter as a gift. After visiting, eating, and reminiscing together, take out your letter and read it with emotion and expression. Let the person gather his or her thoughts and respond. You will be amazed at how wonderful both of you will feel.

MORE BEHAVIORAL PRESCRIPTIONS TO BUILD RESILIENCY

It's not your aptitude, but your attitude that determines your altitude.

—Zig Ziglar, motivational speaker and author

At this point, you have seen 50 Stress Mastery Prescriptions and additional suggestions scattered throughout the chapters. There are certainly many additional stress buffers that you can build into your life to help you maintain resiliency in the face of stressful events, which will undoubtedly come your way. Make a habit of reviewing the action plans at the end of each chapter and following the instructions for keeping on top of your stress and building your resilience.

The 27 additional behavioral prescriptions listed next have each resulted from rigorous scientific studies in the field of stress prevention and stress mastery. Most are prescriptions that you can use in your personal life, and there are six ideas you can present to your administrators for mastering stress in the school setting.

As you know, this book actually includes many more than 77 Stress Mastery Prescriptions. Several of the prescriptions have multiple suggestions and there are many more ideas imbedded in each chapter (for example, Chapter 7 includes 14 creative ideas for bringing fun and humor into your classroom and your life). Don't get overwhelmed by the sheer number of these prescriptions and ideas. You certainly don't have to incorporate all of them into your life to be successful. Pick and choose ones that work well for you. (The entire list of 77 Prescriptions is reproduced in Resource B for easy reference.) Perhaps, try a few new ones each month.

Proven Personal Prescriptions

Connect with people by joining organizations. There are endless examples, from networking and movie clubs to toastmasters and mastermind clubs.

In addition to the relaxation routine described in Resource C, consider a yoga class, meditation, or even self-hypnosis. For the latter, you can learn the power of self-hypnosis by visiting with a licensed psychologist who is certified by the American Society of Clinical Hypnosis.

At bedtime, visualize the most relaxing, pleasurable, serene scene as you drift off to sleep. It could be a real remembrance of a fabulous vacation you took, a childhood memory, or a fantasy place you've dreamt of visiting.

Treat yourself to a massage at least once a month. Soak in a hot tub or sauna regularly.

Continue to endeavor to make new, supportive, nonjudgmental friends all through your life.

Bring more music into your life. Listening to music releases endorphins, which will calm you. Besides making time to listen to your favorite music, take up an instrument, listen to CDs of the sounds of nature. Listen to your favorite music on the way to and from school. Sing along in your car and at home. Go to a karaoke bar and sing to your heart's content.

Make time for satisfying sexual activity in your life. Sexual release is another means of releasing endorphins.

Start a collection or a hobby. Consider painting, pottery, or learning a foreign language. Explore the offerings of your local adult education center or college.

Make a list of things that you enjoy doing that are good for you. These can be solo activities or those enjoyed with family members or a significant other. A simple drive out in the country or to a small town or down by the beach can be very relaxing. Arrange to do at least one each week.

Frequently explore your senses, like walking barefoot on soft grass, wiggle your toes in mud or wet sand, and ride a bike to feel the wind blow through your hair.

Notice color. Research shows that the colors that you surround yourself with directly affect your mood. The three colors that are conducive to relaxation and stress reduction are blue, brown, and pink. Colors to avoid are red, yellow, and green. Use this information in your home decorating, choice of outfits, and classroom colors.

Bring a pet into your life.

Go for rides in the car, without a destination in mind. Explore and enjoy peaceful surroundings. Visit picturesque places and bask in the serenity. Go for nostalgic trips to wonderful places from your childhood or visit your old neighborhood.

Find healthy ways to defuse your frustration or anger on a regular basis. Examples are ballroom dancing, ballet, going to the symphony, getting involved in church activities, going to the gym regularly, and scream to your heart's content at weekend sporting events. If you've always wanted to try something new, just do it—don't find excuses to delay doing it.

In the face of terrible news beyond your control and beyond healing, find a way to deny what you have been told and pray for improvement. Hope for the best every day, but at the same time, let a tiny piece of you prepare for the worst.

If you have children, pay attention to the healthy pleasures of parenting. Plan regular, fun, specific activities with your spouse and children. Be sure to put your family at the top of your priority list.

Be passionate about a mission or purpose in your life and stay focused on it, regardless of detours or roadblocks you run into.

Live in the *now*, as opposed to obsessing about past disappointments or worrying about the future. To do this, you must first allow yourself to enjoy the moment and stop rushing through it. So drive slower, select the longest checkout line and the farthest parking space, smile more at people, and stop checking your watch or clock so often.

Look forward to working on a hobby, and keep a journal or diary of your successes and accomplishments each day.

The average person spends about six weeks a year just looking for things! Organize your space and make sure your desk is neat and orderly before you leave school. Purge your home office of unnecessary clutter. Arrange the things you absolutely need so that you can find them faster, and get rid of everything you're saving for someday reading. Get a lined sheet of paper and print "Things to Do Today" on the top. Make 365 copies so that you can use a new one each day, including both home and school reminders. Check each item off after you complete it.

If you have tried to follow these prescriptions but still feel stressed, depressed, anxious, or afraid, talk to a mental-health professional. Choose a PhD- or PsyD-level psychologist who is licensed in your state and who has been practicing for some time. Preferably, look for a professional with a Cognitive Behavior Therapy specialty. Ask your physicians if they have names of professionals with whom their patients have had good experiences.

Proven In-School Prescriptions

Suggest to your administrators that inservice days should be used to help teachers share stressful experiences in school and brainstorm solutions. Encourage them to provide inservice programs that will have a positive impact on school climate, such as stress management, conflict management, teacher/staff communication skills, and skills for working with upset parents. Suggest that professional-development training include strategies to maintain an *inner calm*, regardless of life's circumstances. Suggest hiring trainers to develop *retreats* for the teachers, administrators, and staff.

Encourage your administrators to provide a quiet space, other than the teacher's lounge, where teachers can find silence and respite during the school day, or where they can enjoy soothing activities, like meditating with soft music or hypnotic recordings. This is a place where teachers can just melt the stress away with a few minutes of relaxation. Posters of serene scenes adorn the walls, and teachers can mentally escape to those places, even for these short breaks in their day. Perhaps refer to this as a "whine and geez" room, where you can complain and feel sorry for yourself all you want.

Form a school-stress committee (including students) at your school (Google Needham, MA, High School for an example). Keep your students' stress low, and your stress will be low. Recommend that your school offer yoga classes, meditation, and stress-management workshops for students. Although your curriculum is jammed already, fitting in these programs will have a major impact on student-teacher stress.

Recommend that your administrators Google the "well-being programme," launched by the Teacher Support Network in Norfolk, England. This is an ideal wellness program that can nip stressors in the bud and teach prevention skills.

Recommend that your administrators provide team-building and job-satisfaction workshops for the teachers and staff. Anonymous surveys can be used prior to the workshops to determine the stress levels of teachers and staff and specific organizational (job-related) stressors that predominate. This whole-school, stress-mastery plan should be an annual or semiannual program for your school.

Recommend that your school put in place a school-based health-care center with a mental-health practitioner on staff. There are currently 1,700 such programs in place across schools in the United States. Such a plan provides for the dual purposes of helping out-of-control students manage their emotions and behaviors while serving as a resource for teachers who are faced with challenging student behavior and other job stressors.

Recall our high school teacher, Mike L. Mike was challenged by 14-hour workdays, difficulty fitting in time with his family, and coming up with innovative ways to keep his students motivated. So how did he maintain his stamina and creativity for so many years and even get nominated to win the *USA Today* prestigious All-USA recognition?

Mike has found that his first priority is to make sure he is smiling as he walks the halls. Sometimes he looks in a mirror to be sure he is smiling, but he is determined not to wear his stress on his face.

Mike loves photography. Therefore, he puts pictures of his students (going back to the beginning of his career) all over his room, and when students pull out a piece of equipment, they are greeted with pictures of students from past years smiling and using that piece of equipment in an activity.

Mike requires his students to do things that will serve them for years to come. For example, he has his students write themselves a letter that speaks to what is happening in their lives, in and out of school. He encourages them to include as many of their classmates in these letters as possible. The students then give these letters to Mike, who holds onto the letters for five years. At the five-year mark, when these students have finished college, he mails the letters to each student. What a pleasant surprise to receive a letter you wrote about what was happening in your life five years ago.

Here are some additional tips from Mike's experience:

1. He stays in shape by riding his bike to and from school each day.

2. Animal-eye dissections are accompanied by opera music playing in the background.

3. He has jokes pinned up all around his classroom and gives credit for students who put physics principles into creative rap songs or "physics carols."

4. He videos his students conducting humorous science projects, for example, the physics police officer arresting people for breaking the laws of physics.

The reason that Mike has been able to maintain his intrinsic motivation over all of these years is that he views his school as representing the "hub of the community." Consequently, Mike views himself as a valued piece of that hub.

In Closing . . . No . . . This is Actually Your Beginning!

Those who identify with success are welcomed by success; those who identify with failure are likewise welcomed by failure . . . the words you choose are the seeds of your future realities.

—Lao Tzu, Tao Te Ching

Richard Carlson's book title *Don't Sweat the Small Stuff . . . and It's All Small Stuff* (1997) sounds patronizing and trite, but his message hits home for most of us, including teachers. The kinds of stressors that teachers deal with on a regular basis are certainly difficult, but they pale in significance to the stressors our ancestors dealt with, as they were forced to hunt down their food and fend off saber-toothed tigers. Yet we turn on the same emergency system inside our brains when we have a difficult parent, student, or administrator to deal with, and our bodies react as if we are running for our lives! As Robert Sapolsky (1998) concludes in his wonderful book, *Why Zebras Don't Get Ulcers*, "In our privileged lives, we are uniquely smart enough to have invented these stressors and uniquely foolish enough to have let them, too often, dominate our lives. Surely we have the potential wisdom to banish their stressful hold" (p. 339).

The wisdom that Sapolsky (1998) implores us to use is the same wisdom found in the well-known Serenity Prayer:

> *God grant me the serenity*
> *To accept the things I cannot change;*
> *Courage to change the things I can;*
> *And wisdom to know the difference.*

It is impossible to avoid all of life's "slings and arrows" and the worry that comes with them. But you can feel heartened by this old proverb: *You cannot prevent the birds of worry and care from flying over your head. But you can stop them from building a nest in your head.*

There are endless choices you can make to live a happier, more productive, and healthier life, both at school and away. You can choose to be a prisoner of your past thinking and belief habits and continue down that road. Or, you can choose to take the road less traveled, starting right now! Today is the time to begin making significant changes in your life. By doing so, your future becomes your present. The essence of this is captured in Portia Nelson's (1993, pp. 2–3) inspirational, metaphoric poem.

Autobiography in Five Short Chapters

by Portia Nelson

Chapter One

I walk down the street.

There is a deep hole in the sidewalk.

I fall in.

I am lost. . . . I am helpless.

It isn't my fault.

It takes forever to find a way out

Chapter Two

I walk down the street.

There is a deep hole in the sidewalk.

I pretend that I don't see it.

I fall in again.

I can't believe I am in this same place.

But, it isn't my fault.

It still takes a long time to get out.

Chapter Three	*Chapter Four*
I walk down the same street.	I walk down the same street.
There is a deep hole in the sidewalk.	There is a deep hole in the sidewalk.
I see it is there.	I walk around it.
I still fall in . . . it's a habit . . . but, my eyes are open.	
I know where I am.	
It is my fault.	*Chapter Five*
I get out immediately.	I walk down another street.

©1993 BY Portia Nelson, from the book *"There's a Hole in My Sidewalk,* Beyond Words Publishing, Hillsboro, OR.

So please choose to walk down another street—not by leaving your noble profession of teaching—but by identifying and changing the habits that have kept you feeling overwhelmed, stressed, and unhappy. And remember, even if you are not as passionate about your profession as you hoped you'd be, you can still feel passionate about your life. Carol Orsborn (1994), the brilliant author of books based on I Ching, the 3,000-year-old work of wisdom, puts it succinctly: "Where to begin? Sing in a bathtub. Tap-dance while the computer prints out. Treat yourself to the rarest cheese on the shelf. Take every opportunity to jump out of yourself and into humor, openness, perspective, and faith" (p. 184).

ACTION PLAN FOR STRESS MASTERY

Table 8.4	Action Plan for Stress Mastery

Check off when completed.	
New Behavior	*What I Did and the Date Accomplished*
❑ Every day I will examine negative events in my life and determine whether I am interpreting what happened to me in an optimistic or pessimistic way. ❑ ❑	What I did:
❑	Date accomplished:

New Behavior	*What I Did and the Date Accomplished*
❏ I will practice the A-B-C-D-E method of developing optimistic thinking. ❏ ❏ ❏	What I did: Date accomplished:
❏ I will revisit the Thinking-Pattern Worksheet (TPW) and use it to practice developing of optimistic thinking. ❏ ❏ ❏	What I did: Date accomplished:
❏ Twice a month, I will review the list of Stress Mastery Prescriptions in Resource B and choose one to add to my ongoing practice of building my resilience. ❏ ❏ ❏	What I did: Date accomplished:

REFERENCES

Bristol, C. M., & Sherman, H. (1987). *TNT: The power within you.* New York: Simon & Schuster.

Carlson, R. (1997). *Don't sweat the small stuff . . . and it's all small stuff.* New York: Hyperion.

Frost, R. (1993). *The road not taken and other poems.* New York: Dover.

Haven, B. Q., Frandsen, K. J., Karren, K. J., & Hooker, K. R. (1992). *The health effects of attitudes, emotions, relationships.* Provo, UT: EMS Associates.

Nelson, P. (1993). *There's a hole in my sidewalk.* Hillsboro, OR: Beyond Words.

Orsborn, C. (1994). *How would Confucius ask for a raise?* New York: Morrow.

Peterson, C., & Bossio, L. M. (1993). Healthy attitudes: Optimism, hope, and control. In D. Goleman & J. Gurin (Eds.), *Mind body medicine: How to use your mind for better health* (pp. 351–366). Yonkers, NY: Consumer Reports Books.

Sapolsky, R. (1998). *Why zebras don't get ulcers.* New York: Freeman.

Seligman, M. E. (1998). *Learned optimism.* New York: Pocket Books.

Seligman, M. E. (2002). *Authentic happiness: Using the new positive psychology to realize your potential for lasting fulfillment.* New York: The Free Press.

Siegel, B. S. (1986). *Love, medicine & miracles.* New York: HarperCollins.

Siegel, B. S. (1998). *Peace, love & healing.* New York: Harper & Row.

Sobel, D. S., & Ornstein, R. (1996). *The healthy mind healthy body handbook.* New York: Patient Education Media.

Resource A

Glossary of Acronyms

CHAPTERS 1, 4, AND 5

SNS (sympathetic nervous system): This is frequently referred to as the fight-or-flight nervous system. The SNS switches on whenever people sense danger, but it also switches on whenever people even think about something that worries or bothers them. Once the SNS is activated, the body goes into emergency mode, and this leads to a spike in strain symptoms, including muscle tightening and blood pressure elevation. Because we can learn to control our thinking, we can ultimately learn the trigger thought patterns that we habitually use, which ultimately switch on the SNS and cause our strain. Once we understand those patterns, we can learn how to avoid triggering the SNS.

CHAPTER 2

LCUs (life-change units): These point totals attribute to each event on the RLCQ. The more LCUs one accumulates in a 12-month period, the greater the probability of stress-related illness or emotional difficulties befalling that person in the next 12 months.

RLCQ (Recent Life Changes Questionnaire): This is a researched-based, 70-event questionnaire that helps you to determine how many *stress points* you have accumulated because of the changes you have made in the last 12 months. The more points you have, the greater probability that you are suffering from stress-related symptoms. Keeping track of your stress points over any 12-month period helps you make important decisions to modify the changes you make in your life during the next 12 months.

CHAPTER 4

CHD (coronary heart disease): Cited by the American Medical Association as the most important modern health problem in the United States, where each year more than half a million Americans die from coronary heart disease (Roskies, 1987).

CHAPTERS 5 AND 8

A-B-C-D-E model: This is an easy way to understand the process of stress provocations and how to avoid stress outcomes. *Activating* events **(A)**, *beliefs* about those events **(B)**, and *consequent* emotions and behaviors **(C)**, can be modified by *disputing* thoughts **(D)**, leading to *energized*, revitalized *emotions* **(E)**.

TPW (Thinking-Pattern Worksheet): This chart organizes your thoughts, the self-defeating thinking pattern you habitually use, and the disputing thoughts that will eliminate or prevent stress outcomes.

CHAPTER 6

The three Cs of hardiness (commitment, control, and challenge): These are the primary determinants of psychological hardiness or stress resistance. Once you learn to develop or increase these traits in your own life, you will make a giant leap toward ultimately buffering yourself from the impact of stress.

REFERENCE

Roskies, E. (1987). *Stress management for the healthy type A.* New York: Guilford Press.

Resource B

77 Behavioral Prescriptions to Master Your Stress and Build Your Resilience

PROVEN PERSONAL PRESCRIPTIONS

Stress Mastery Prescription 1: *Take care of your emotional health by taking care of your physical health. Consider visiting a licensed naturopathic physician to learn about foods and natural supplements that have been proven to reduce and prevent stress. The following are examples of physical features that have been shown to directly impact moods and stress levels: keep your blood sugar low with frequent, smaller meals that include protein; eat light at night; get ample sleep; avoid alcohol, caffeine, and tobacco; load up on antioxidant-rich foods, and keep your weight in the normal range for your age and height.*

Stress Mastery Prescription 2: *Practice breathing through your diaphragm. Put your hands on your stomach and breathe deeply so that your hands move out when you inhale and move back in when you exhale. If your hands are not moving and only your shoulders and chest move when you breathe deeply, you are engaging in shallow, less relaxing breathing. You can easily teach yourself to breathe through your diaphragm with practice.*

Stress Mastery Prescription 3: *Recognize that you can live with a certain amount of stress in your life and that it may even be beneficial to you.*

Ask yourself what calm people do to maintain their stress levels. Examples of answers to that question are jogging or walking each morning before work, making time for lunch each day with a calm friend or colleague, and reading articles or the rest of this book on how to master the stresses in life.

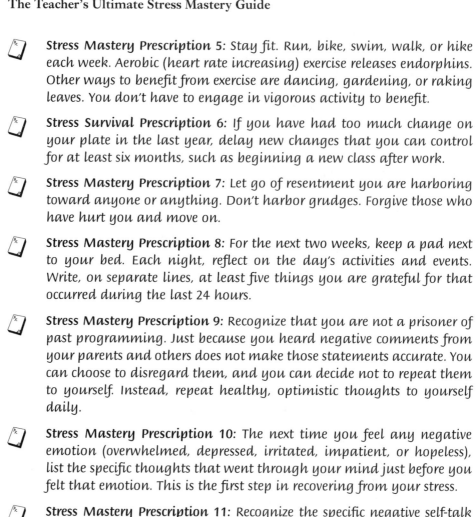

Stress Mastery Prescription 5: *Stay fit. Run, bike, swim, walk, or hike each week. Aerobic (heart rate increasing) exercise releases endorphins. Other ways to benefit from exercise are dancing, gardening, or raking leaves. You don't have to engage in vigorous activity to benefit.*

Stress Survival Prescription 6: *If you have had too much change on your plate in the last year, delay new changes that you can control for at least six months, such as beginning a new class after work.*

Stress Mastery Prescription 7: *Let go of resentment you are harboring toward anyone or anything. Don't harbor grudges. Forgive those who have hurt you and move on.*

Stress Mastery Prescription 8: *For the next two weeks, keep a pad next to your bed. Each night, reflect on the day's activities and events. Write, on separate lines, at least five things you are grateful for that occurred during the last 24 hours.*

Stress Mastery Prescription 9: *Recognize that you are not a prisoner of past programming. Just because you heard negative comments from your parents and others does not make those statements accurate. You can choose to disregard them, and you can decide not to repeat them to yourself. Instead, repeat healthy, optimistic thoughts to yourself daily.*

Stress Mastery Prescription 10: *The next time you feel any negative emotion (overwhelmed, depressed, irritated, impatient, or hopeless), list the specific thoughts that went through your mind just before you felt that emotion. This is the first step in recovering from your stress.*

Stress Mastery Prescription 11: *Recognize the specific negative self-talk patterns you have developed. Make a list of common negative thoughts you have in a typical day and check the list of 10 common distorted-thinking patterns to determine which ones you engage in regularly.*

Stress Mastery Prescription 12: *Whenever you recognize that you are upset and thinking negatively, use the quick reference guide of questions to challenge that negative thinking.*

Stress Mastery Prescription 13: *Review Table 4.1, Checklist of Potential Type-A Behaviors, to see if you fit this profile.*

Stress Mastery Prescription 14: *Simplify your life. Ask yourself what really needs to be done. If you don't perform a specific task right now, what's the worst that will happen? Get a good Spam blocker so you can avoid having to read the bulk of your e-mails, and be selective regarding the number of people to whom you give your e-mail address. Read Lakein's How to Get Control of Your Time and Your Life (1973).*

Stress Mastery Prescription 15: *Learn to be flexible and just go with the flow. As the Quaker proverb goes, "In the face of strong winds, let me be a blade of grass. In the face of strong walls, let me be a gale of wind"* (Sapolsky, 1998, p. 416).

Stress Mastery Prescription 16: *The next time you feel any negative emotion, revisit Table 4.1 to see if you are engaging in these behaviors.*

Stress Mastery Prescription 17: *Become aware of the triggers to your stress feelings.*

Stress Mastery Prescription 18: *Find a relaxation technique you're comfortable with, and make it part of your daily routine. See Resource C for a relaxation example. Practice your relaxation skills in a place where you will be left alone and not interrupted by the phone, TV, or other people.*

Stress Mastery Prescription 19: *Use short relaxation exercises several times a day.*

Stress Mastery Prescription 20: *Get in touch with your false beliefs and change them.*

Stress Mastery Prescription 21: *Recognize the price you are paying to achieve more and more in less and less time.*

Stress Mastery Prescription 22: *Get a time-management book, and practice the techniques you learn from it.*

Stress Mastery Prescription 23: *Never skip or shorten breakfast.*

Prescription 24: *Take multiple minibreaks during the day.*

Stress Mastery Prescription 25: *Break up your work routine by taking the time to go for a walk, meditate, or listen to soothing music or your relaxation routine on your iPod or portable CD player.*

Stress Mastery Prescription 26: *Make a deal with yourself that you will never leave school later than 5:00 p.m. (unless you have an additional duty).*

Stress Mastery Prescription 27: *Try hard to eliminate multitasking.*

Stress Mastery Prescription 28: *Pay attention to your angry and hostile behaviors, and learn to modify them using anger-mastery techniques.*

Stress Mastery Prescription 29: *Practice active-listening techniques.*

Stress Mastery Prescription 30: *Review the people-pleasing behaviors in Table 4.2 to see if you fit this profile.*

Stress Mastery Prescription 31: *Learn how to assert yourself without feeling guilty.*

Stress Mastery Prescription 32: To help you recognize your assertiveness choices, use the form in Table 4.9 and describe each situation where you had a choice but behaved nonassertively.

Stress Mastery Prescription 33: Take notice of and keep a record of situations in which you were assertive and reward yourself accordingly.

Stress Mastery Prescription 34: Catch yourself whenever you are awfulizing and stop it immediately, using the TPW.

Stress Mastery Prescription 35: The next time you feel any negative emotion (e.g., overwhelmed, frightened, depressed, irritated, impatient, hopeless), do the following: Use the TPW and describe the event that led to the emotions; write down the specific emotions you feel and rate them. Write down the automatic thoughts that preceded you feeling those emotions, and determine which distortion patterns those thoughts fit. Then write down rebuttal thoughts that make sense. Believing those rebuttal thoughts should help you feel better.

Stress Mastery Prescription 36: When you don't have time to use the TPW, use the thought-stopping, calming-breathing, write-it-down, or worry-time techniques.

Stress Mastery Prescription 37: Don't try to control that which cannot be controlled or things that have already happened. Stick with what you are capable of controlling in the present.

Stress Mastery Prescription 38: Make a list of your short- and long-term goals, **right now**, and answer the eight questions listed in Table 6.3 for each goal.

Stress Mastery Prescription 39: To develop attitudes of hardiness, and to stick to your goals, start using positive affirmations daily. Write down or record your affirmations and read or listen to them at least 10 times a day for a minimum of 21 days.

Stress Mastery Prescription 40: Watch comedies on TV, and go to lighthearted, fun movies. Avoid the-sky-is-falling world news reports on TV and in the papers. Be selective in what you decide to watch on TV or at the theater. Ask yourself beforehand, "Is this show positive, upbeat, and life affirming, or is it negative, downbeat, and sure to leave me feeling worse?"

Stress Survival Prescription 41: Seek out every opportunity to belly laugh yourself to health.

Stress Mastery Prescription 42: Whatever seems unbearable or embarrassing today will be hilarious down the road. Tell yourself, "Someday, I'll be laughing about this."

Stress Mastery Prescription 43: Find creative ways to bring fun and humor to your classroom.

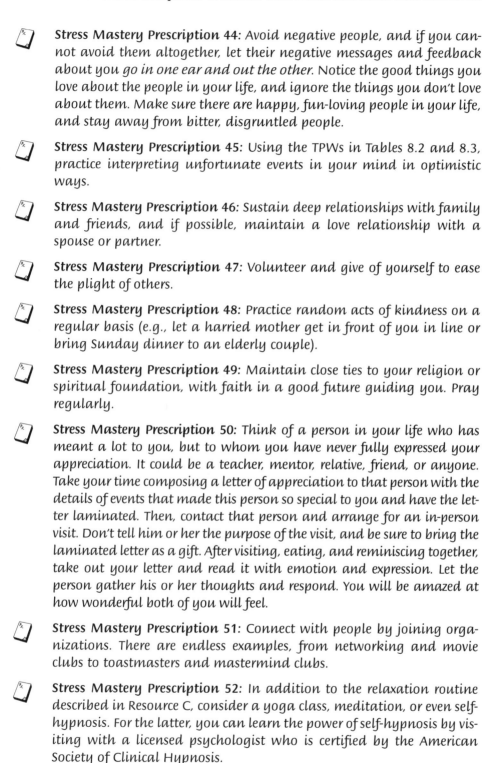

Stress Mastery Prescription 44: Avoid negative people, and if you cannot avoid them altogether, let their negative messages and feedback about you *go in one ear and out the other.* Notice the good things you love about the people in your life, and ignore the things you don't love about them. Make sure there are happy, fun-loving people in your life, and stay away from bitter, disgruntled people.

Stress Mastery Prescription 45: Using the TPWs in Tables 8.2 and 8.3, practice interpreting unfortunate events in your mind in optimistic ways.

Stress Mastery Prescription 46: Sustain deep relationships with family and friends, and if possible, maintain a love relationship with a spouse or partner.

Stress Mastery Prescription 47: Volunteer and give of yourself to ease the plight of others.

Stress Mastery Prescription 48: Practice random acts of kindness on a regular basis (e.g., let a harried mother get in front of you in line or bring Sunday dinner to an elderly couple).

Stress Mastery Prescription 49: Maintain close ties to your religion or spiritual foundation, with faith in a good future guiding you. Pray regularly.

Stress Mastery Prescription 50: Think of a person in your life who has meant a lot to you, but to whom you have never fully expressed your appreciation. It could be a teacher, mentor, relative, friend, or anyone. Take your time composing a letter of appreciation to that person with the details of events that made this person so special to you and have the letter laminated. Then, contact that person and arrange for an in-person visit. Don't tell him or her the purpose of the visit, and be sure to bring the laminated letter as a gift. After visiting, eating, and reminiscing together, take out your letter and read it with emotion and expression. Let the person gather his or her thoughts and respond. You will be amazed at how wonderful both of you will feel.

Stress Mastery Prescription 51: Connect with people by joining organizations. There are endless examples, from networking and movie clubs to toastmasters and mastermind clubs.

Stress Mastery Prescription 52: In addition to the relaxation routine described in Resource C, consider a yoga class, meditation, or even self-hypnosis. For the latter, you can learn the power of self-hypnosis by visiting with a licensed psychologist who is certified by the American Society of Clinical Hypnosis.

Stress Mastery Prescription 53: At bedtime, visualize the most relaxing, pleasurable, serene scene as you drift off to sleep. It could be a real *remembrance of a fabulous vacation you took, a childhood memory, or a fantasy place you've dreamt of visiting.*

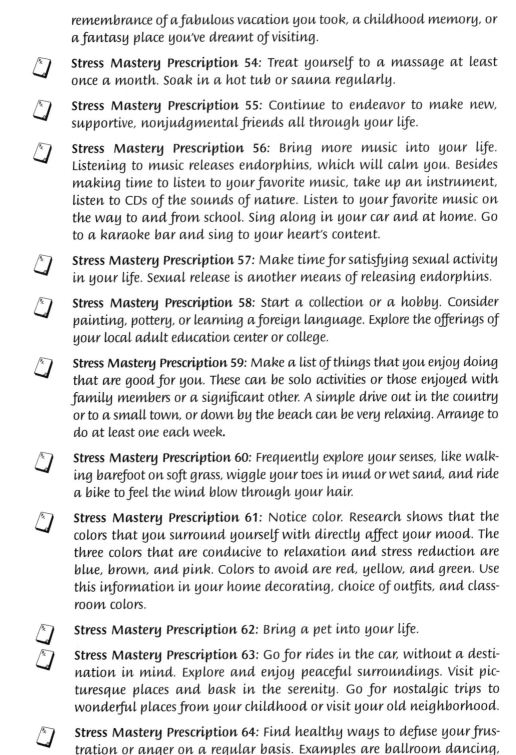

Stress Mastery Prescription 54: Treat yourself to a massage at least once a month. Soak in a hot tub or sauna regularly.

Stress Mastery Prescription 55: Continue to endeavor to make new, supportive, nonjudgmental friends all through your life.

Stress Mastery Prescription 56: Bring more music into your life. Listening to music releases endorphins, which will calm you. Besides making time to listen to your favorite music, take up an instrument, listen to CDs of the sounds of nature. Listen to your favorite music on the way to and from school. Sing along in your car and at home. Go to a karaoke bar and sing to your heart's content.

Stress Mastery Prescription 57: Make time for satisfying sexual activity in your life. Sexual release is another means of releasing endorphins.

Stress Mastery Prescription 58: Start a collection or a hobby. Consider painting, pottery, or learning a foreign language. Explore the offerings of your local adult education center or college.

Stress Mastery Prescription 59: Make a list of things that you enjoy doing that are good for you. These can be solo activities or those enjoyed with family members or a significant other. A simple drive out in the country or to a small town, or down by the beach can be very relaxing. Arrange to do at least one each week.

Stress Mastery Prescription 60: Frequently explore your senses, like walking barefoot on soft grass, wiggle your toes in mud or wet sand, and ride a bike to feel the wind blow through your hair.

Stress Mastery Prescription 61: Notice color. Research shows that the colors that you surround yourself with directly affect your mood. The three colors that are conducive to relaxation and stress reduction are blue, brown, and pink. Colors to avoid are red, yellow, and green. Use this information in your home decorating, choice of outfits, and classroom colors.

Stress Mastery Prescription 62: Bring a pet into your life.

Stress Mastery Prescription 63: Go for rides in the car, without a destination in mind. Explore and enjoy peaceful surroundings. Visit picturesque places and bask in the serenity. Go for nostalgic trips to wonderful places from your childhood or visit your old neighborhood.

Stress Mastery Prescription 64: Find healthy ways to defuse your frustration or anger on a regular basis. Examples are ballroom dancing, ballet, going to the symphony, getting involved in church activities, going to the gym regularly, and scream to your heart's content at weekend sporting events. If you've always wanted to try something new, just do it—don't find excuses to delay doing it.

Stress Mastery Prescription 65: In the face of terrible news beyond your control and beyond healing, find a way to deny what you have been told and pray for improvement. Hope for the best every day, but at the same time, let a tiny piece of you prepare for the worst.

Stress Mastery Prescription 66: If you have children, pay attention to the healthy pleasures of parenting. Plan regular, fun, specific activities with your spouse and children. Be sure to put your family at the top of your priority list.

Stress Mastery Prescription 67: Be passionate about a mission or purpose in your life and stay focused on it, regardless of detours or roadblocks you run into.

Stress Mastery Prescription 68: Live in the *now*, as opposed to obsessing about past disappointments or worrying about the future. To do this, you must first allow yourself to enjoy the moment and stop rushing through it. So drive slower, select the longest checkout line and the farthest parking space, smile more at people, and stop checking your watch or clock so often.

Stress Mastery Prescription 69: Look forward to working on a hobby, and keep a journal or diary of your successes and accomplishments each day.

Stress Mastery Prescription 70: The average person spends about six weeks a year just looking for things! Organize your space and make sure your desk is neat and orderly before you leave school. Purge your home office of unnecessary clutter. Arrange the things you absolutely need so that you can find them faster, and get rid of everything you're saving for someday reading. Get a lined sheet of paper and print "Things to Do Today" on the top. Make 365 copies so that you can use a new one each day, including both home and school reminders. Check each item off after you complete it.

Stress Mastery Prescription 71: If you have tried to follow these prescriptions but still feel stressed, depressed, anxious, or afraid, talk to a mental-health professional. Choose a PhD- or PsyD-level psychologist who is licensed in your state and who has been practicing for some time. Preferably, look for a professional with a Cognitive Behavior Therapy specialty. Ask your physicians if they have names of professionals with whom their patients have had good experiences.

PROVEN IN-SCHOOL PRESCRIPTIONS

Stress Mastery Prescription 72: *Suggest to your administrators that inservice days should be used to help teachers share stressful experiences in school and brainstorm solutions. Encourage them to provide inservice programs that will have a positive impact on school climate, such as stress management, conflict management, teacher/staff communication skills, and skills for working with upset parents. Suggest that professional-development training include strategies to maintain an* inner calm, *regardless of life's circumstances. Suggest hiring trainers to develop* retreats *for the teachers, administrators, and staff.*

Stress Mastery Prescription 73: Encourage your administrators to provide a quiet space, other than the teacher's lounge, where teachers can find silence and respite during the school day, or where they can enjoy soothing activities, like meditating with soft music or hypnotic recordings. This is a place where teachers can just melt the stress away with a few minutes of relaxation. Posters of serene scenes can adorn the walls and teachers can mentally escape to those places, even for these short breaks in their day. Perhaps refer to this as a "whine and geez" room, where you can complain and feel sorry for yourself all you want.

Stress Mastery Prescription 74: Form a school-stress committee (including students) at your school (Google Needham, MA, High School for an example). Keep your students' stress low, and your stress will be low. Recommend that your school offer yoga classes, meditation, and stress-management workshops for students. Although your curriculum is jammed already, fitting in these programs will have a major impact on student-teacher stress.

Stress Mastery Prescription 75: Recommend that your administrators Google the "well-being programme," launched by the Teacher Support Network in Norfolk, England. This is an ideal wellness program that can nip stressors in the bud and teach prevention skills.

Stress Mastery Prescription 76: Recommend that your administrators provide team-building and job-satisfaction workshops for the teachers and staff. Anonymous surveys can be used prior to the workshops to determine the stress levels of teachers and staff and specific organizational (job-related) stressors that predominate. This whole-school, stress-mastery plan should be an annual or semiannual program for your school.

Stress Mastery Prescription 77: Recommend that your school put in place a school-based health-care center with a mental-health practitioner on staff. There are currently 1,700 such programs in place across schools in the United States. Such a plan provides for the dual purposes of helping out-of-control students manage their emotions and behaviors while serving as a resource for teachers who are faced with challenging student behavior and other job stressors.

Resource C

A Deep-Muscle Relaxation Technique

Place yourself on your most relaxing chair, bed, or couch. Make sure that you will not be disturbed or interrupted for the next 15 minutes or so. Turn your phones, TVs, and radios off. When you listen to this recording, do not listen in a place where your attention will be required, such as while driving a car.

Now, read this script into a recorder slowly, in a very calm and monotone voice. Either use your own voice or ask someone whose voice is soothing and calming to record it. You can use a digital recorder, from which you can either burn a CD or put it directly on your iPod. If you prefer a cassette, just record it into a cassette recorder and you can play it on a Walkman with headsets. When recording these scripts, go slowly and pause wherever you see the dots (. . .).

I am getting in a very comfortable position, a position either on a bed, a couch, or on a comfortable chair . . . a position that is going to be perfect for me with no distractions, no phones ringing, and no people trying to get my attention. . . . I will block everything out of my mind that might get in the way of focusing my concentration completely and totally on the task at hand. . . . I will give myself an opportunity to get into a relaxed state, which will raise my overall level of peacefulness and calm. I can even give myself some suggestions to remain calm even under the most trying circumstances on my job, for example.

Professional singers and musicians have learned that the most powerful form of breathing during their performances is through their diaphragms. That method not only brings in more oxygen, but also quickly relieves excess tension. Now, I can learn to do the same thing . . . so easily. The way I'll know when I am truly breathing through my diaphragm is that when I inhale deeply, my stomach actually pushes out, and when I exhale, my stomach area actually comes back in.

I can practice this by simply folding my hands over my stomach . . . then take in a deep, deep breathe . . . and now let it out. If my stomach pushed out when I breathed in, that's the correct breathing technique, but if mainly my chest and shoulders were moving when I breathed in, that is not the best form of relaxed breathing.

So as I am silent for the next few moments, I will just practice making my stomach expand out as I breathe in and have it go back in when I breathe out. I can easily check this by watching my folded hands over my stomach. I take a deep breath in and let it out. I will practice this for a few minutes.

Pause now for a few minutes and let the recorder run while you practice breathing through your diaphragm.

(Continue talking here)

I know that I can easily practice this technique every night when I lie down to go to sleep by simply folding my hands and resting them on my stomach, and then practice expanding my stomach every time I breathe in and relaxing my stomach every time I breathe out. I breathe in, expanding my stomach . . . and breath out, relaxing my stomach.

I now focus my concentration completely and totally on my left hand. As I focus on my left hand, I make a fist with that hand. . . . I feel the tension. . . . I understand that feeling of tension. . . . And now I relax and notice the difference in sensations between tension and relaxation. I notice how much more comfortable and calming it is when I allow that tension to disappear and dissolve away.

Once again, I make a tight fist with my left hand. . . . I feel the tension, in my fist, writs, and up my arm. . . . And now, I relax my fist . . . allowing the tension to disappear and dissolve away, allowing it to be replaced by calm, comfortable, enjoyable, relaxed muscular sensations.

Now, I move the focus of concentration to my right hand, and as I do so, I make a tight fist with my right hand. . . . I feel the tension in my right fist, my hand, and my arm. . . . I understand that feeling. . . . I allow the tension to increase tremendously. . . . And now . . . I relax my right hand, completely and totally.

Again, I notice the difference in the sensations between tension and relaxation, and I notice how much more comfortable and calming it is when I allow the tension to disappear and dissolve away . . . and replace it with calm . . . comfortable . . . enjoyable . . . relaxed muscular sensations.

Once again, I make a tight fist with my right hand. I feel the tension. . . . I allow that tension to build. . . . And now I relax. I let the tension disappear and dissolve away . . . replacing the tension in my fist with calm, comfortable, enjoyable, relaxed muscular sensations.

Now, I move the focus of my concentration to both of my arms. As I concentrate on my arms, I stretch them out in front of me as far as

I can. . . . I feel that tension and understand that feeling. I relax again. . . . I notice the difference in sensations between tension and relaxation, and I notice how much more comfortable and calming it is when I allow the tension to disappear and be replaced by loose . . . limp . . . calm . . . comfortable muscular sensations in my arms.

Once again, I stretch my arms out in front of me. I feel the tension involved. . . . I allow the tension to build. . . . And now . . . I relax. The tension dissolves away and disappears and is replaced by calm, comfortable . . . loose . . . limp muscular sensations.

Now, I move the focus of concentration to my shoulders. As I concentrate on my shoulders, I shrug them up as if I am going to touch my ears. . . . I feel that tension all the way through my shoulders, my upper back, and my neck muscles. . . . And now . . . I relax. Again, I notice the difference between the tension and the relief, as I let those muscles get loose and limp. . . . I feel calm, comfortable, and completely relaxed.

Once again, I shrug my shoulders up. . . . I feel the tension in my upper back, as I am forcing my shoulders up toward my ears. . . . And now . . . I relax. All the tension that was there is disappearing and dissolving away, and it is being replaced with calm . . . comfortable . . . enjoyable . . . relaxed . . . muscular sensations.

Now, I move the focus of my concentration to my forehead and scalp. As I think about my forehead and scalp, keeping my eyes closed, I raise my eyebrows as high as I can and feel the creases across my forehead and scalp. . . . And now, I relax my forehead and scalp muscles. I notice the wonderful sensations, as I allow my forehead and scalp to smooth out and feel calm . . . comfortable . . . and completely relaxed.

Again, I raise my eyebrows, causing creases across my forehead and scalp. . . . And now I relax. All of the tension that was there disappears and dissolves away and is replaced by calm . . . comfortable . . . enjoyable . . . relaxed . . . smooth . . . muscular sensations.

NOTE: If you are wearing contact lenses, skip the next section on relaxing your eye muscles.

Now, I concentrate on my eyes. As I concentrate on my eyes, I close them as tightly as I can. I feel that tension. . . . I understand that feeling. . . . And now, I relax my eye muscles . . . allowing that tension to disappear and dissolve away . . . replacing it with calm . . . comfortable . . . enjoyable . . . relaxed . . . muscular sensations.

Once again, I close my eyes tightly. . . . I feel the tension. . . . And now, I relax. All of the tension disappears and dissolves away and is replaced by calm . . . comfortable . . . enjoyable . . . relaxed . . . muscular sensations.

NOTE: If you wear a retainer in your mouth, have braces, or any problems with your teeth or jaws, skip the next section on relaxing your mouth and jaw muscles.

Now, I move the focus of concentration to my mouth, and as I concentrate on my mouth, I clench my teeth shut as tightly as I can. . . . I feel the tension throughout my facial and jaw muscles . . . I understand that feeling. . . . And now, I relax my teeth, feeling loose and limp. . . . My jaws are feeling calm, comfortable, and completely relaxed.

Once again, I clench my teeth shut tightly. . . . And I relax. I notice the difference in sensations between tension and relaxation. I notice how much more calming it is when I let my jaw muscles get loose and limp . . . feel calm . . . comfortable, and completely relaxed.

Now, I focus my concentration on my neck. . . . As I concentrate on my neck, I turn my head to the left as far as I can. And now I turn to the right . . . now down into my chest. . . . And now, I relax. All of the muscles of my neck are getting loose and limp. . . . They're feeling calm, comfortable, and completely relaxed.

Once again, I turn my head to the left . . . and now to the right . . . now down into my chest . . . and relax. I feel complete and total relaxation . . . almost as if the muscles of my neck are like ropes that have been tied in knots, and these knots are now unraveling and leaving loose, limp, calm, comfortable muscular sensations. Loose, limp, calm, comfortable muscular sensations.

Now, I focus on my breathing. I imagine that I'm inside my body, listening to my breathing. I listen to how deeply I breathe. . . . I listen to how rapidly or slowly I breathe. . . . I notice that as I take slower, deeper breaths, it's much more relaxing and calming. As I take slower . . . deeper breaths . . . it's much more relaxing and calming.

Now, I take a nice deep breath and hold it, just holding the tension . . . letting it all gather in my lungs. . . . And now I exhale. What a sense of release, as all of the tension is leaving my body . . . completely and totally. Once again, I take a nice deep breath. . . . I feel the tension . . . and exhale all of that tension away, leaving in its place calm . . . comfortable . . . relaxed . . . muscular sensations. Calm . . . comfortable . . . relaxed . . . muscular sensations. I know that every time I want to relax deeply, I can give myself a series of slow, deep breaths . . . hold it each time . . . let the tension build . . . and then exhale. I breathe in . . . hold it . . . and now breathe out . . . allowing all of the tension to dissolve away . . . completely and totally. As I breathe in . . . through my nose . . . and out through my mouth . . . I feel the relaxation getting deeper and deeper. Every time I breathe in . . . through my nose . . . and out through my mouth . . . I feel the relaxation growing . . . deeper and deeper.

Now, I move the focus of concentration to my stomach. As I focus on my stomach, I pull my stomach muscles in as far as I can. Now I relax my stomach muscles. . . . I let the tension disappear and dissolve away, and I allow my stomach muscles to get completely and totally relaxed. . . . Once again, I pull my stomach muscles in, feel the tension . . . and relax. All of the tension in my stomach muscles disappears and dissolves away . . . being replaced by calm, comfortable, relaxed, loose, limp muscular sensations.

Still focusing on my stomach, I do the opposite. I push my stomach muscles out. . . . And I feel that tension. . . . Now, I relax. I notice the difference. . . . I notice how much more comfortable and calming it feels to just let go. Once again, I push my stomach muscles out. . . . I feel the tensions. . . . And now . . . I relax all of those muscles . . . calm, comfortable, relaxed muscular sensations.

Now, I focus on my buttocks and my thighs. I squeeze my buttocks and thigh muscles, and I feel the tension in the lower part of my body. . . . Now, I relax. . . . Once again, I squeeze my buttocks and thigh muscles . . . and I relax. All of the tension in my lower body is dissolving away and disappearing and being replaced by calm . . . comfortable . . . relaxed . . . muscular sensations.

Now, I concentrate on my legs and feet. I stretch my legs and feet out, pointing my toes away from me and stretching my feet out as far as I can. I feel that tension and notice how that feels. And now, I relax. I dissolve away that tension completely and totally . . . replacing it with loose . . . limp . . . calm . . . comfortable . . . relaxed muscular sensations. Loose . . . limp . . . calm . . . comfortable . . . muscular sensations. Such a good feeling . . . such a relaxing feeling. . . Once again, I stretch my legs and feet out, pointing my toes away from me . . . I feel that tension and notice how that feels. And now, I relax. I dissolve away that tension completely and totally . . . replacing it with loose . . . limp . . . calm . . . comfortable . . . relaxed muscular sensations.

I continue my slow, deep, relaxing breathing, and I tell myself that with each deep, satisfying breath I take, I feel relaxation spreading from my scalp down my face across my eyes . . . past the bridge of my nose . . . across my mouth . . . down into my neck . . . and across my shoulders . . . all the way down my arms to my wrists and to my fingers . . . down through my chest and my stomach . . . down my back . . . to my lower trunk . . . down through my thighs to my knees . . . legs . . . ankles . . . feet . . . and toes.

As I continue to relax . . . deeper and deeper . . . I clear away all worries, concerns, and distractions. . . . That's right . . . just allowing my eyes to comfortably close now, if they haven't already closed. And I can stay in this relaxed state as long as I wish.

I know that my mind may drift off to a relaxing memory, a peaceful and serene place that I have visited in the past. Perhaps I will remember a wonderful and calming experience that I had sometime in my childhood . . . perhaps a favorite family vacation or a special place that my friends and I used to go to . . . perhaps in the woods or a tree hut . . . or at the beach . . . or in the snow. It doesn't really matter what memory comes to mind. What does matter is that I just allow my mind to drift as I listen to my own soothing voice describing this place. . . .

Now just describe the scene that comes to mind . . . The place, the season, the time of day, where you are, who, if anyone, is with you, what you are doing, the weather, the aromas, the colors, the breeze, what you hear and see, and anything else you can recall.

Perhaps I can already feel relaxed comfortable sensations entering my shoulder or a leg or an arm, as I listen to my voice describing this favorite scene. Perhaps I can briefly focus on any sounds that may be around me, in this room, at this very moment . . . like a ticking clock or the distant murmur of traffic. . . . Although I may hear these sounds occasionally as I focus on my voice, they only serve to lull me into an even deeper state of relaxation and comfort.

I wonder if I can recall other experiences of drifting off. Perhaps being so completely engrossed in a movie or TV show that I lost track of every-one in the room . . . lost track of all the sounds made by these people, and perhaps I only paid attention to those sounds once the show ended. Perhaps a favorite song comes to mind from my past, bringing me another memory that is so soothing and comforting, and perhaps the music is in the background now, as I listen to my voice drifting deeper and deeper.

Peaceful and quiet feelings flow through me right now . . . so relaxed and peaceful. Perhaps the music lingers in the background, and my con-scious mind is drifting off to another place . . . another time. There is no need for me to make this happen. . . . It just happens. Although there is cer-tainly no need to understand how these wonderful feelings develop or why they develop, I just flow with it . . . absorb it. Perhaps I notice my breathing, and how it changes to slow, deep breathing. I know that deep relaxation can take many forms . . . from heavy feelings, to light, floating feelings, and to warm or tingly sensations. It doesn't matter which I feel. . . . They all represent relaxation.

I don't know if my mind will begin by relaxing just one of my fingers, or perhaps it will choose a shoulder or a leg to begin with. My mind can focus on the parts of my body that are beginning to relax, or it can drift off to another place. . . . It's up to me. My mind will continue the process of relaxing my entire body, perhaps randomly, perhaps in a pattern begin-ning with the top of my head making its way all the way down to the tips of my toes. With every word I say, I'm feeling the relaxation flowing deeper and deeper throughout my body.

Pause here for a minute or two, letting the recorder continue to record the silence.

It is now time to come back across time and space, to here and now. I shall count from one to five, and as I do so, I will come back to here and now, awake and alert. **One** . . . **two** . . . coming back across time and space . . . **three** . . . . stretching my muscles now . . . becoming fully alert and awake but remaining relaxed, confident, and excited about my ability to relax myself on command . . . **four** . . . free from old scripts and fears and knowing that every single time I listen to this recording, I will get stronger and stronger, more and more self-assured, able to deal with any challenges that come along . . . and **five**. . . . fully awake, wide alert, fully refreshed. I open my eyes now, fully awake, refreshed, and alert.

Resource D

Web Site Resources on Classroom Management

You can begin your Web-site search of resources by going to the wonderful series of sites provided by the American Psychological Association's Center for Psychology in Schools and Education (APA, CPSE) at http://www.apa.org/ed/cpse/homepage.html.

Here are excellent sites for learning how to use highly successful, research-based, practical classroom-management techniques:

- http://www.nea.org/tips/manage/behavior.html

  This is the National Association of Education's (NEA) Web site that focuses on classroom management. It is part of the Works4Me tips library. It is a compilation of teacher-submitted tips on noise control, staying on task, safety issues, transforming behavior, discipline referrals, and tracking behavior.

- http://www.nea.org/classmanagement/archive.html

  This is another section of the NEA Web site, which has a long list of archived strategies and offers practical advice that pertains to many situations.

- http://www.teachingideas.co.uk/more/management/contents.htm

  These are brief postings on classroom-management suggestions from primary-level teachers in the United Kingdom. Because the ideas were generated by teachers, they are practical and may easily be adopted in classrooms.

- http://www.myceconline.org/phpBB2/

  The Council for Exceptional Children maintains discussion forums on various topics. The behavior and discipline forum is the most popular and includes over 200 topics related to classroom management with over 1,000 posts. There is also a new-teacher exchange.

- http://www.education-world.com/a_curr/archives/classmanagement.shtml

  This archives a long list of articles on classroom discipline. The articles range from examinations of what to do midyear, to revisiting classroom rules, to academic choice, and dealing with bullies.

- http://scholar.google.com/

  This is a search engine for scholarly works on the Web, and it provides a gateway to refereed articles (in scholarly journals) on any given topic. As many of the articles are available as full-text, it offers quick access to valuable information. One may type in, "self-monitoring classroom behavior," "classroom management," "classroom discipline," or "self-regulation classroom" and find lists of related articles.

  The three PBIS Web sites provide excellent resources to gain an overview of the model and suggestions for implementation. These three PowerPoint presentations are highly recommended:

- www.pbis.org/files/George/c00206c.ppt

  (Classroom management: Systems and practices)

- www.pbis.org/files/George/c00206a.ppt

  (Schoolwide positive behavior support: Getting started)

- www.pbis.org/files/Horner/apbs0306bxspec.ppt

- www.interventioncentral.com

  This Web site, by Jim Wright, provides a very useful list of reinforcers and offers free tools to help school staff and parents promote positive classroom behaviors and foster effective learning for all children. Topics include how to reduce problems by increasing effectiveness of academic instruction, the good behavior game, and behavioral contracts.

- http://www.jimwrightonline.com/php/jackpot/jackpot.php

  Another Jim Wright Web site, this is an online reinforcer generator survey. There is no charge for using it. The online reinforcer generator survey provides a list of reinforcers and allows to you select age-appropriate items as well as insert reinforcers that you think might be of interest to the child. You may customize the form so the child's name appears and direction.

- http://teachers.net/wong/

  This is a monthly newsletter written by Harry and Rosemary Wong on various aspects of classroom management. The topics focus on what a teacher should do prior to the start of the school year, objectives for the first days of school, greeting students, and motivating students. Much of the content is based on Wong's 2004 book *The First Days of School: How to Be an Effective Teacher.*

- http://education.indiana.edu/~safeschl/

  The Indiana University Safe and Responsive Schools Project is a model demonstration and technical assistance project funded by the U.S. Department of Education; dedicated to enabling schools and school districts develop a broader perspective on school safety and violence prevention; and stressing comprehensive planning, prevention, and parent/community involvement.

Index

CORWIN

A SAGE Company

The Corwin logo—a raven striding across an open book—represents the union of courage and learning. Corwin is committed to improving education for all learners by publishing books and other professional development resources for those serving the field of PreK–12 education. By providing practical, hands-on materials, Corwin continues to carry out the promise of its motto: **"Helping Educators Do Their Work Better."**

ONTARIO
PRINCIPALS'
COUNCIL

The Ontario Principals' Council (OPC) is a voluntary professional association for principals and vice-principals in Ontario's public school system. We believe that exemplary leadership results in outstanding schools and improved student achievement. To this end, we foster quality leadership through world-class professional services and supports. As an ISO 9001 registered organization, we are committed to our statement that "quality leadership is our principal product."